The Popcorn Millionaire and Other Tales of Saugatuck

by Kit Lane

Pavilion Press
P.O. Box 250
Douglas, Mi 49406

Copyright 1991
By Pavilion Press

All Rights Reserved

ISBN 1-877703-20-6

LC # 91-060187

Amelia Earhart's letters from camp, now preserved in the Schlesinger Library, Radcliffe College, are used with the permission of Muriel Earhart Morrissey, Amelia's next of kin.

Cover: The cover drawings are by Saugatuck artist Sylvia Randolph. The front cover, drawn from an old photograph, shows the ballroom in the Big Pavilion shortly after its grand opening in 1909.

Table of Contents

George F. Root:
The First Resorter 5

Susan B. Anthony:
For Women's Rights 9

Mrs. Mary A. Livermore:
Women's Rights II 21

George W. Maher:
Prairie on the Lakeshore 30

Carl Sandburg:
Guest Lecturer 42

D. K. Ludwig:
The Popcorn Millionaire 48

Amelia Earhart:
A Summer at Camp 61

Ignace Jan Paderewski:
Lakeshore Serenade 71

George Coutoumanos:
Greek Poet 76

Thor Heyerdahl:
Visit to Harbor View 83

Robby Benson:
Debut at the Red Barn 86

Saugatuck has been a center of settlement and civilization for more than 200 years. Its varied history and activity has produced a list of famous people with an area connection that continues to grow.

Some (suffragette Susan B. Anthony and pianist Paderewski) were famous when they arrived here; others (Carl Sandburg, Amelia Earhart, and Robby Benson) attained their prominence after they left the area.

Future millionaire D.K. Ludwig and Greek poet George Coutoumanos are the only ones recorded here who could truly be called residents. Others (George F. Root and George W. Maher) were summer visitors, or invited guests (Thor Heyerdahl and Paderewski). One of the famous personages whose story is narrated here never arrived at all (Mrs. Mary A. Livermore).

In doing research for this book more celebrities were discovered than could be contained in a single volume. A future Saugatuck tales book will include James Fenimore Cooper, Edgar Lee Masters, F. B. Stockbridge (who founded the Grand Hotel on Mackinac Island), Thomas Eddy Tallmadge (architect for Colonial Williamsburg and the Saugatuck Woman's Club Auditorium), Sunday school publisher David C. Cook, Christian writer E. Stanley Jones, puppeteer Burr Tillstrom and others.

The Saugatuck area has always been a special place. Native Americans were attracted to the plentiful game by the Kalamazoo River and the towering dune near its mouth. Settlers were drawn by business opportunities, and dreams of wealth. Resorters sought cool shores and pleasant diversion. The attraction (some would call it "spell") of Saugatuck continues. As one young summer visitor explained, "Saugatuck isn't like other places. It's, well... you know, different."

Kit Lane

GEORGE F. ROOT
The First Resorter

In the summer of 1871 Saugatuck had one of the first indications that perhaps there would be a future for the town, even after the timber was cut.

According to William A. Taylor, the son of the Rev. J. F. Taylor, pastor of the Saugatuck Congregational Church from 1868 to 1877, one Sunday a strange couple appeared in his father's church. They were recognized at once as city people by their clothes. The man wore a silk hat and carried a gold trimmed cane. The couple was ushered into a pew occupied by several boys, including young Taylor.

Shortly after the service a gold-headed cane was found in the pew and the pastor's son was asked to return it to its owner, a task readily accomplished as the only strangers in town were easily located. The cane proved to belong to George F. Root, singer, composer and pioneer music publisher from Chicago, and he has by tradition been designated Saugatuck's first "resorter."

George Frederick Root was born in Sheffield, Massachusetts, in 1820, into a musical family. His father was a singing school master, and young George was named for 18th century composer, George Frederick Handel. In 1844 he became a teacher of music in New York City and in 1853 founded the New York Normal Institute, especially for training teachers of music. He was the composer of cantatas, sacred music and a number of popular songs including "Rosalie, the Prairie Flower" and "There's Music in the Air." Text and lyrics for many of his cantatas and songs were written by Fanny Crosby, who had been a pupil of Root's when he taught at the New York School for the Blind. Blind from infancy, she was later to become a very prolific and famous hymn writer. Her better-known works include "Blessed Assurance," "Rescue the Perishing," and "Pass Me Not, O Gentle Savior."

George F. Root

Root's best known works were the battle songs he wrote during the Civil War, especially "Tramp, Tramp, Tramp the Boys are Marching," "The Battle Cry of Freedom," and "Just Before the Battle, Mother." There were many incidents related of lagging spirits buoyed when the men sang one of Root's songs. Charles A. Dana, editor of the *New York Sun*, and a member of Lincoln's cabinet, wrote: "George Root did more to preserve the Union than a great many Brigadier-Generals, and quite as much as some brigades. His songs were a great force in the homes of the people as well as among the men in the field. They touched the chords of patriotism as they had never been touched before."

In addition to writing and composing, Root was part of the firm of Root & Cady of Chicago which conducted a general music trade, publishing sheet music for the local market, until they found a national market for their patriotic songs during the Civil War. When Root visited Saugatuck in the summer of 1871 he could not have foreseen that the firm would be virtually wiped out in the great Chicago fire of October, 1871.

The summer of 1871 was a fairly prosperous one for the Saugatuck area. The population of the Great Lakes area was growing and business enterprises were beginning to flourish. There was, at last, a growing market for the lumber and other wood products that were created in Saugatuck mills and the leather produced by the tanneries. Fruit farming had recently been introduced to the area. At first, the average farmer with a surplus of fruit sold it to local markets or to the crews of visiting ships. Later, as the output of their orchards increased, farmers expanded their markets to include the rapidly growing populations in Chicago and Milwaukee. The fire that burned the warehouse of the Root & Cady music publishing firm in 1871 also brought one of the busiest and most lucrative periods to Western Michigan. The demand for wood and leather products needed for the rebuilding of Chicago and for other Midwestern towns destroyed, or seriously damaged, in the series of fires the same day taxed Saugatuck mills to capacity. Some mills ran 24 hours, and through the winter to take advantage of the booming market. Although this increased productivity brought in money at an unprecedented rate for a while, it also hastened the day when there would be no more timber to cut, forcing the area to seek other commercial enterprises.

The Roots visited Saugatuck at least one more time, the following year. His son, Charles T. Root, wrote a letter dated

March 7, 1873, to Pastor Taylor referring to Mr. Root's remembrance of the "pleasant weeks passed in Saugatuck during the two preceding summers." In 1935 when Rev. Taylor's son found the letter among his father's papers he wrote the *Commercial Record* identifying Mr. and Mrs. Root as early summer visitors, perhaps, even, the first true vacationers that the area hosted. Root died in 1895.

His hymn, "The Shining Shore," carries an image that may have a Saugatuck inspiration.

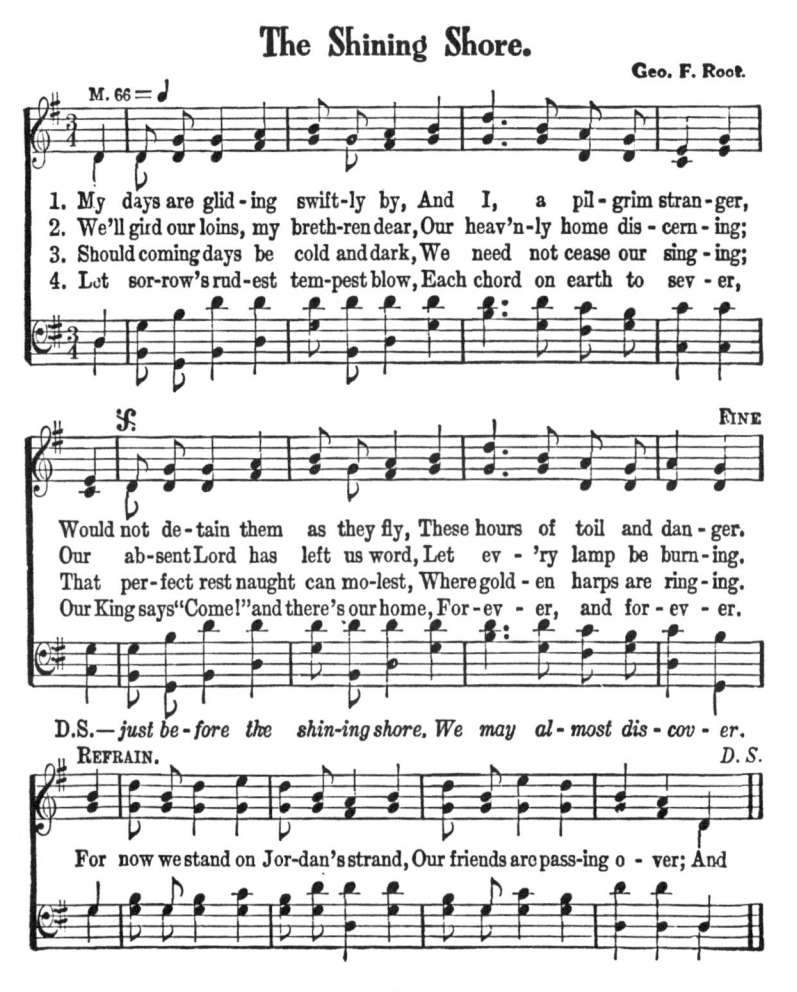

The Shining Shore.

Geo. F. Root.

1. My days are glid-ing swift-ly by, And I, a pil-grim stran-ger,
2. We'll gird our loins, my breth-ren dear, Our heav'n-ly home dis-cern-ing;
3. Should coming days be cold and dark, We need not cease our sing-ing;
4. Let sor-row's rud-est tem-pest blow, Each chord on earth to sev-er,

Would not de-tain them as they fly, These hours of toil and dan-ger.
Our ab-sent Lord has left us word, Let ev-'ry lamp be burn-ing.
That per-fect rest naught can mo-lest, Where gold-en harps are ring-ing.
Our King says "Come!" and there's our home, For-ev - er, and for-ev - er.

D.S.—*just be-fore the shin-ing shore, We may al-most dis-cov-er.*

REFRAIN.

For now we stand on Jor-dan's strand, Our friends are pass-ing o - ver; And

SUSAN B. ANTHONY
For Women's Rights

In March of 1879 Susan B. Anthony had a scheduled lecture in Grand Rapids at Powers Opera House, which met with indifferent success, especially in the eyes of the Grand Rapids newspaper editor who reported under the headline "Spinster Susan's Suffrage Show":

"A 'miss' of an uncertain number of years, more or less brains, a slimsy figure, nut cracker face and store teeth goes raiding about the country attempting to teach mothers and wives their duty. This is Susan B. Anthony... She turns up her somewhat ill-shaped proboscis at tobacco, in whose favor so great a man as Bulwer has said: 'A pipe! It is a great soother, a pleasant comforter...' Having snuffed out tobacco, Susan launches a tirade at whisky, and having disposed of this, the Chinese, Negro and school question, she returns to her revels and gets in the finishing shoulder hits on man... And so this mild mannered woman represents the 'rights' portion of her sex, and makes men glad that they have always voted 'no' on the question of extending the suffrage to them."

At some point during her stay in the state Miss Anthony was approached by Mrs. Tamar (Phillips) Moore, the wife of Horace D. Moore, an early saw mill owner, to come to Saugatuck. There was apparently little advance planning, and only about a week's notice. The February 28, 1879 issue of the *Lakeshore Commercial* noted at the top of its Local Matters column: "Susan B. Anthony is coming."

About mid column a paragraph read: "Miss Susan B. Anthony to deliver her great lecture, "Woman Wants Bread, Not the Ballot," at this place soon. Exact date will be given next week."

Susan B. Anthony about 1860

The March 7 issue also had two separate paragraphs in the local news columns. The first read, "Come out next Wednesday night and hear the most Famous woman in America." The second got down to the specifics:

"Susan B. Anthony will deliver her celebrated lecture, "Woman Wants Bread, Not the Ballot," at Morrison's Hall next Wednesday evening under the auspices of the Saugatuck Lecture Association. Tickets 25 cents, children under 12 years, 15 cents. Tickets are for sale at the post office and the stores of A. B. Taylor, F. A. Winslow, C. E. Wells, C. E. Bird, C. Whitney, D. L. Barber, Saugatuck, and at the post office and MacLean's Drug Store, Douglas. If those living in Douglas who wish to attend will leave their names at the post office or at MacLean's Drug Store a team will call for them."

According to an account published in the 70th anniversary history of the Saugatuck Congregational Church in 1930, which was written by one of the Moore daughters, Mrs. Wenona Sherwood of Allegan, Miss Anthony stayed with the Moores at their house near the river just north of Saugatuck. The daughter wrote that the famous lecturer was in the area for two weeks, which would have been an unusually lengthy stop on a speaking tour. One-nighters were more common. During her stay Mrs. Moore, Miss Anthony and others "made a house to house canvass which satisfied the women that the time was propitious to organize."

The newspaper mentions only one meeting and in the March 14 issue, following the lecture which was held Wednesday, March 12, 1879, the editor wrote. "The lecture given by Miss Susan B. Anthony at Odd Fellows Hall on Wednesday evening was all that could be expected. The audience was the largest we have seen in Saugatuck for many years and every one seemed to enjoy it very much. Miss Anthony is a fine speaker and has a clear ringing voice so that she could be heard distinctly in very part of the house. She thoroughly understands her subject and is laboring zealously for the woman suffrage cause of which she is an able expounder."

A second assessment of the speech was written by Saugatuck correspondent J. F. Henry in the *Allegan Journal*. He commented with remarkable detachment: "The lecture by Susan B. Anthony drew together such an audience as is seldom seen in Saugatuck. The hall was crowded and the several votes taken demonstrated that the talented speaker carried her hearers with her."

The Congregational church history reports that "evening meetings were held in the old town hall and were well patronized. Each night Miss Anthony addressed the assemblage. She, delicate of stature, extremely effeminate in manner, dressed in man's attire, would seem ludicrous but she was shown every respectful courtesy and was successful in closing six of the fourteen saloons then in operation."

The comment on her dress is surprising. Although many editors, and a few of her friends, have written that she was not very particular about her clothing, no other source has mentioned that at this stage in her speaking career she wore anything that might have been construed as man's apparel. One of the Grand Rapids editors noted, "She was plainly attired and her appearance would not cause remark in a crowd." Certainly if she had worn anything like men's pants the writer who described her "nut cracker face" could not have resisted some comment on her garments.

Beginning about 1850 many of the leaders of the women's movement, Susan B. Anthony included, had tried to popularize the wearing of the "bloomer costume." In a move to make women's dress more practical and sanitary they replaced the voluminous street-sweeping skirts with a shorter dress, which terminated at the lower end of the calf, and underneath it wore full trousers cut in Turkish style and made of black broadcloth. Many women also wore fewer undergarments, discarding the whalebone corsets of the day, and topped the outfit off with a full Spanish cape. The new dress was designed by Elizabeth Smith Miller, and named for Mrs. Amelia Bloomer who promoted it in her newspaper, *The Lily*.

The intention was to "free women from the bondage of cumbersome clothing," and make the home safer, by lessening the possibility that the homemaker might trip on her dress on the stairs with household items or a child in her arms. The outfit was considered too revealing, but, as one contemporary editor pointed out, the main thing it revealed was "the hitherto suppressed fact that woman is a biped." The suffragettes had largely given up the costume by 1855 because it proved an unnecessary distraction to their main message. They were accused of wanting not only man's vote, but his pants as well. However, a cartoon published in 1873 in *The Daily Graphic*, a New York newspaper, shows Miss Anthony attired in a shorter skirt and tailored bloomers under the caption "The Woman Who Dared". Apparently the question of attire was not entirely dead by this time, and perhaps she occasionally wore her bloomer costume, especially in the chill of a Michigan March.

"The Woman Who Dared"

She also sometimes wore rather tailored jackets which might appear man-like to a young girl. This may be what the Moore daughter remembers.

There is some confusion about the site of the meeting (or meetings). The advance story in the *Commercial Record* states that Miss Anthony was expected to speak at Morrison's Hall, a second floor auditorium in downtown Saugatuck on Butler Street about where the Elms Hotel (later the Petter Gallery) was built. The Odd Fellows Hall, where the newspaper account of the meeting said that the talk was actually held was in the same block, but at the southwest corner of Mason and Butler Streets, above Flint's Store. The Odd Fellows Hall was less than a year old having been dedicated in October of 1878. It was larger and it could be that the meeting was moved there when advance ticket sales indicated that more space was needed.

Tamar (Phillips) Moore

The Congregational Church history's contention that the meetings were held in the old town hall cannot be accurate. The Saugatuck Village Hall was not built until 1880, but was near enough and similar in structure to Morrison's Hall that the two halls might easily have been confused in retrospect. It is also likely that official village board meetings were held at Morrison's Hall, making it a de facto town hall.

A group of ladies met the week following the lecture ("as a consequence of Miss Anthony's visit" the *Allegan Journal* noted) at the residence of Mrs. Moore to organize a Woman's Christian Temperance Union "auxiliary and co-operative with the W.C.T.U. of the state." In quick succession a White Ribbon Club (for those who vowed not to drink alcohol), a Red Ribbon Club (for those who were vowed to give it up and signed a pledge), and a Blue Ribbon Club (for juveniles only) were organized.

The church history reports that Miss Anthony personally tied a Red Ribbon in the buttonhole lapel of each man who signed the pledge.

The Moore house was one of the older homes in the area, having been built in the early 1860's by Horace D. Moore near his mill north of Saugatuck, at a community sometimes called Mooreville. Prior to 1880 a portion of the grounds was fenced and deer were kept in the park-like enclosure, hence the house and grounds were often called the Park House. The building still stands in 1991 and is operated as a Bed and Breakfast. It is now within the city boundaries of Saugatuck, on the old road to Holland.

Susan B. Anthony was a life-long advocate of temperance, but by 1879 she had decided that needed reforms could not be achieved by a strictly temperance or religious movement, but only through extending the voting privilege to women. She earned both her reputation and her living on the lecture circuit. It was her method of operation to write, edit, and polish, a speech over a fairly long period, and then to embark on a tour giving the same memorized speech in each city with little variation. Each time she started a tour she would have to write a new speech.

The Moore House from an 1880 county history.

"Woman Wants Bread, Not the Ballot," was actually an old speech when it was delivered in Michigan having been succeeded by "The Homes of Single Women." However, the new speech was not a popular success and she often reverted to her favorite old standby when she was visiting an area for the first time. She wrote despairingly of the new lecture, "It is stale, flat and unprofitable. I do not believe I shall ever be able to make but one satisfactory speech and that is my Bread and the Ballot."

The lecture tour of 1878-79 was arranged by the Slayton Bureau. For her appearances she received $30 a night. The tour began in October of 1878 in New Hampshire and Vermont, where Miss Anthony traversed the roads between towns by sleigh. She then moved through New York and Pennsylvania and into the Middle West, traveling chiefly by train, covering Michigan, Illinois, Ohio, and Indiana, and dropping down into Kentucky for the first time. The tour ended in May of 1879 with a suffrage meeting in St. Louis, Missouri.

After her speech in Grand Rapids on March 4, she moved on to Kalamazoo where she was scheduled to lecture at 8 p.m. March 10, at Union Hall. In the next day's *Daily Telegraph* the editor wrote: "Susan B. Anthony appeared at Union Hall last evening but the elementary strife which prevailed without at the hour of the opening of Susan's speech within, had the effect to keep back the people who might otherwise have come to hear and be made wise. So she did not lecture at all." The "elementary strife" was a thunderstorm.

Prior to her appearance in Saugatuck she had delivered the same lecture March 11 in Allegan at Empire Hall (located on the northwest corner of Hubbard and Locust Streets prior to the 1884 fire). The Allegan editor seemed far less reluctant to discuss the details of the talk than his Saugatuck counterpart and in the March 15 *Allegan Journal* wrote:

"Empire hall was well filled Tuesday evening to hear this famous woman upon her first visit to Allegan. Her discourse can scarcely be called a lecture as it was mainly composed of a disconnected series of incidents she had witnessed, anecdotes she had heard, and experiences she had passed through during the mystical number of years she had been the leading champion in the field of woman suffrage. Those who attended, misled by the title of her lecture, expecting to hear some good logical reason why all the opportunities and careers available to the masculine sex should not be thrown open to women as bread winners, must have been grievously disappointed.

"The lady in opening announced that 'Woman wants bread, not the ballot,' and wanted the comforts, luxuries, and all the good things of life, but as essential to procuring these, and superior to everything in achieving the perfect happiness of woman, was the possession of the franchise. From this point no more was heard about woman's need of daily bread, but the speaker passed from the great bread riots of the laborers in London fifty years ago, to the abuses and degradation to which the Chinaman in California to-day is subjected, and showed, as she claimed, that the only remedy for these evils lay in enfranchising their victims. She denounced the anti-Chinese bill in unmeasured terms as infamous and perfidious, and caused the most earnest applause of the evening when she praised the president for placing his veto thereto. She condemned all trade unions and said in no single instance had they done good; though sometimes accomplishing their object in the temporary advance of wages, that was an object not worth fighting for, as it could not be held without possessing the ballot.

"Miss Anthony said that she heard it continually said that the grange movement was a dead failure, but when she traveled over railroads in Iowa one year ago at three cents per mile, where nine years before she paid five cents, she thought it had accomplished a part of its object, and even if it had not attained it fully, while it being the first instance under the sun where men took their wives, sisters and daughters and placed them politically on an equal footing with themselves, no praise was too high for it.

"The speaker talked in an off-hand manner for almost two hours and a half without hesitation, and referred to no notes but carried statistics and all 'in her head.' Her way of taking up collections to advance 'the cause' at the close of lectures for which she is paid and which others pay to hear, is reprehensible and should be discountenanced. There is no good reason why man should deny woman the ballot if she wishes it for he can not tell where he rightfully gets the power to withhold it from her; but this desired result is not hastened in its arrival by the talk of such scolds as Miss Anthony, even though she couples with her tirades much that is true and admirable."

Some of the above assessment was a thinly rewritten version of the account of her Grand Rapids lecture in the *Grand Rapids Daily Eagle* of March 4, but there is enough new material to indicate that the Allegan editor had actually attended the speech.

The Allegan writer did refrain from commenting on her personal appearance, a popular theme of her detractors. Looking today, at pictures of Susan B. Anthony, she appears to the modern eye quite ordinary, not beautiful, but not especially ugly either. However, something in her manner must have rubbed reporters, particularly male reporters, the wrong way for they would write: "No longer is she in the bloom of youth -- if she ever had any bloom -- hardfeatured, guileless, cold as an icicle. . . " and "She is above the medium height for women, dresses plainly, is uncomely in person, rather coarse, rugged features and masculine in manners."

In Saugatuck there was a real attempt at cracking down on the saloons which remained open. Saturday, March 15, the day after Miss Anthony's main speech, probably while she was still in town, Saugatuck Village Marshal E. S. Pride filed a complaint against the Globe Saloon, owned by Charles Miller, charging that he was open after 11 o'clock thereby violating a village ordinance. The following day the Marshal filed charges against S. Clipson, for not closing his brewery on Sunday.

The cases came to a jury trial on March 27, at Odd Fellows Hall in Saugatuck, the same site where Susan B. Anthony had spoken two weeks earlier. Both defendants were found not guilty. J. F. Henry, explained the Miller case in the *Allegan Journal*:

"The Marshal testified that he entered Miller's saloon at eight minutes past eleven and notified him that it was after closing time. Miller replied that by his watch it wanted ten minutes of eleven, but that he would obey orders and close up. He accordingly, did so, shutting the door but keeping a lamp burning. The marshal took up a position on the opposite side of the street and watched the premises. Twenty minutes after he had ordered Miller to close up he saw parties go to the door, knock and gain admittance. At twenty-five minutes of twelve he rapped at Miller's back door and informed him that his saloon was not closed within the meaning of the law, and that he should lodge complaint against him. The prosecution had subpoenaed two witnesses, expecting to prove by them that they had seen the door of the place open after eleven o'clock; but these parties had no knowledge of the hour, did not carry watches, and could not tell whether it was before or after eleven. . . Mr. Miller said that he regulated his watch by Brandstetter the jeweler's time. The latter is said to be regulated by taking observations of the sun. Pride regulates his watch by post-office time which is corrected daily by telegraph from Chicago. Of course correct Saugatuck time would be some minutes ahead of Chicago time, and if Brandstetter's time was correct by the sun, then Miller's watch should have been some minutes faster than Pride's instead of twenty minutes slower."

The Holland paper gives the fullest account of the Clipson charge. "Four persons were found in the brewery. The defendant claimed that being a cold day he was obliged to go into the brewery to make a fire, as he would otherwise have lost a brewing of beer that was in the process of manufacture." Others joined him, but all gave testimony that "they saw no beer there and none was sold or had there by any person." One young witness caused much amusement by testifying that he would not have touched the stuff if it had been offered, declaring that he would rather drink sour milk than beer.

Although Susan B. Anthony returned to Michigan many times on lecture tours, and for meetings, there is no record that she ever spoke again in Saugatuck. Mr. and Mrs. Moore sold their home and left the area in 1885. Susan B. Anthony died in 1906 at the age of 86 without seeing her dream of female suffrage become the law of the nation. The vote was finally extended to women nationwide with the ratification of the 19th amendment in 1920.

MRS. MARY A. LIVERMORE
Women's Rights II

A lecture by Mrs. Mary A. Livermore, "The Coming of Man," scheduled for Odd Fellows Hall, in January of 1882 was less successful. Mrs. Livermore had been touted in the local paper as "the greatest woman lecturer on the American stage," but in the January 20 issue the editor reported:

"Mrs. Livermore is a fraud. At least that is the opinion held by the majority of Saugatuckians. She was engaged for a lecture here last Monday night, and came as far as Richmond where a special and comfortable conveyance was in waiting to bring

Mrs. Livermore traveling by train

her over to Saugatuck. The trip of six miles was made in thirty minutes, but this dainty advocate of women's rights could not stand that much exposure unless she could have a closed carriage. The day was not a stormy one and any woman in ordinary health, could have rode that distance without hurt. Mrs. Livermore's action in the matter was positively dishonorable and she should be held responsible for the loss to the Saugatuck Lecture Association. Had she failed to make railroad connections not a word of fault would have been found; but she came to the station, left the train, and refused to come in a comfortable carriage because it was not a close one. She has no business in the lecture field, when she can break engagements as deliberately and dishonorably as she has this one. By her course she has cheated our Association out of at least fifty dollars. This is the second lecturer engaged of the Redpath Lyceum Bureau of Chicago who has broken with us this winter; the first, Mrs. Dainty and the second Mrs. Livermore. We advise our sister towns to give these ladies the go-by in the future. Certain it is that Saugatuck will never give either of them another bid."

In the *Allegan Journal* it was the lead story of the January 20 issue: "From all we can learn, Mrs. Livermore treated Saugatuck people with great disrespect Monday evening, and broke her contract, by refusing to go from Richmond to Saugatuck in an open carriage. A large audience gathered to hear her and they were sorely disappointed and highly indignant. The weather was mild, the roads good, and the carriage a fine one, but uncovered. That it lacked a cover was the only reason she gave for putting her baggage back on the train and leaving. She has been held in very high esteem here for supposed excellent personal qualities as well as her worth as a lecturer, but this incident will go far toward creating a different feeling."

The Saugatuck column in the *Journal* was headlined, "A Ride Mrs. Livermore Declined," and said "Many came in from the country in the evening and were indignant that for so slight a cause Mrs. Livermore should break her engagement."

The Douglas reporter, D.C., in the same paper added one more detail to the story: "We understand that Mrs. Livermore was met at Richmond by a gentlemen from Saugatuck with an open conveyance and that on this ground she refused to come, rejoined the train and went on to Grand Rapids. It has been reported further to D.C., that she transmitted by telegraph a message to Saugatuck, signifying her wish for a covered conveyance. D.C. wishes to pass no judgement on the subject as this is all he has heard, and this only by report."

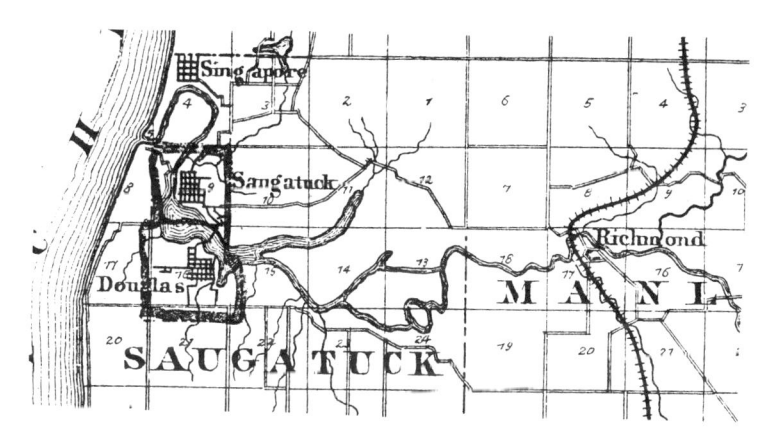

The road from Saugatuck to Richmond was about six miles long in this 1873 map, along the Old Allegan Road.

Mary Ashton (Rice) Livermore was a contemporary of Susan B. Anthony. They were both born in 1820, Mrs. Livermore in Boston. She was married in 1845 to the Rev. Daniel Parker Livermore a Universalist pastor, and husband and wife edited *The New Covenant*, a church periodical, in Chicago, 1857-69. During the Civil War she nursed in hospitals from Cairo to New Orleans, and helped to organize several veteran's aid associations. She and Jane Hoge organized the Great Northwestern Sanitary Fair in Chicago in 1863 which netted more than $85,000 for the Union Army. President Abraham Lincoln sent the original draft of the Emancipation Proclamation to be auctioned off. (Acquired by Chicago interests it was lost in the 1871 fire.) Mary Livermore was an outspoken suffrage supporter and editor of *The Agitator*, a newspaper sponsored by the Union Woman Suffrage Society, and later the *Woman's Journal* into which it merged. For much of the battle to win women the vote she and Susan B. Anthony were on slightly different sides of the question (one group advocated approaching the question on the federal level, the other was content to go state by state) but they were great personal friends and sometimes crossed boundaries to support one another.

Mrs. Livermore had a greater diversity of topics. She spoke on women's suffrage, and temperance, when requested, but had other choices for other audiences. Although self-taught, she had a dynamic and dramatic speaking style that her audiences seemed to enjoy. In describing her temperament, her good friend, Lilian Whiting, writing in 1915 in her book, *Women Who Have Ennobled Life*, commented: "Mrs. Livermore, like all persons who have great qualities, had also the defects of her qualities. A strong will may sometimes be unduly insistent; a forceful temperament, with its intense power for effectiveness, may have undue vehemence; and patience is one of the things that such a temperament has to learn."

The week prior to her engagement at Saugatuck one of the Grand Rapids papers noted that she had lectured in Cincinnati on the 8th. "She speaks at Saugatuck next Monday evening, and at the Baptist Church Tuesday evening in the Y.M.C.A. course, and at Big Rapids Wednesday night." The editor went on to praise her as a "matronly woman and eloquent lecturer with distinct enunciation, correct pronunciation, artistic emphasis, scholarly culture and earnestness of purpose."

The settlement of Richmond was located in Manlius Township on the Kalamazoo River. In the mid-1830's John Allen (best known in Michigan as one of the founders of Ann Arbor) and others, had attempted to found a milling town on the north bank of the river. The project died in the economic depression of 1837, and several years later another attempt at settlement was made on the south side of the river. A bridge across the river at this point was built in 1842 giving the project some economic impetus. It was further boosted by the construction of the railroad in 1871 which crossed the Kalamazoo River just downstream from the highway bridge. The town was usually called Richmond on the maps, but when a post office was applied for in 1872 it was discovered that there was already a Richmond in Michigan (in Macomb County between Port Huron and Detroit) and the post office was officially designated New Richmond. Later, the name came to be applied to the entire settlement. In the summertime travelers who left the train at Richmond were sometimes conveyed to Saugatuck by riverboat.

In 1882 there were two daily scheduled express trains to Richmond, a regular stop on the Chicago and Lake Michigan Railroad. The train Mrs. Livermore most likely took was the day express which was scheduled to reach Richmond at 2:55 in the afternoon. The night train stopped there at 4:45. The stop at Richmond, located on the Kalamazoo River 15 minutes by rail north of Fennville, and 25 minutes south of Holland, was usually very brief, just long enough to drop off and pick up passengers. The decision by Mrs. Livermore not to go to Saugatuck in the uncovered carriage would have been made very quickly. If she then reboarded the train, there would have been little time for discussion. This early hour would have given sufficient time for word of the canceled lecture to spread in the villages of Saugatuck and Douglas, but there was too little time to give notice to the people on the outlying farms. Telephone service to the area did not begin until 1896.

Assuming that the lecture organizers in Saugatuck received Mrs. Livermore's request for a closed, or covered carriage, there is a strong possibility that they were unable to comply because there was none available. Winter scenes taken of Saugatuck's Butler Street about the turn of the century, show the hitching racks lined with carriages and sleighs, none of them covered. At least one of the area doctors had a buggy, with some protection on three sides, but covered and enclosed carriages were not very practical on the heavily wooded roads of Western Michigan.

Mrs. Livermore spoke on Tuesday night in Grand Rapids, but no mention was made in any of that city's newspapers of her failure to meet her obligation in Saugatuck the previous night. Her speech at Grand Rapids was, "The Boys of To-day," on the influence exerted upon the youth of America of that time. She was familiar to Grand Rapids audiences having spoken there on seven different occasions beginning in 1869.

Although the *Grand Rapids Eagle* reporter noted that her speech was "full of good advice and pertinent illustrations," Mrs. Livermore was less kindly handled by the *Times* editor, probably the same writer who had described Miss Anthony's "slimsy figure" and "nut cracker face." His account of the lecture began:

"The Times is not prejudiced in favor of women on the platform. As Solomon wrote: 'As a jewel of gold in a swine's snout so is a fair woman without discretion.'

"The Times fancies that women who roam over the land looking after lyceums, associations, and what not, instead of attending to their own homes, are, as a rule, 'without discretion.'

"We have no feeling against Mrs. Livermore in person. As the lady grows older she becomes more temperate in her remarks and conservative in her opinions. We have never heard her deliver a lecture so good as was that last evening. Matter and manner, generally speaking, were excellent.

"The church was full and the people -- being of a class which does not attend the theatre regularly and so is easily amused -- laughed heartily and enjoyed the stale wit and oft-used expressions falling from the good woman's lips. . . ."

In 1897 Mrs. Livermore wrote her autobiography, *The Story of My Life or The Sunshine and Shadows of Seventy Years*. Although there is no mention of the Saugatuck incident she devotes an entire chapter to the subject of "Keeping Lecture Engagements Under Difficulties," and bragged, "I have always been very punctilious in keeping my engagements, and doubt whether any lecturer has disappointed audiences less frequently than myself."

The chapter includes an illustrated account of a lecture in Cincinnati, which may have been the one just preceding the Saugatuck engagement. Because no one had come to take her to the station Mrs. Livermore missed her train. When she telegraphed the committee in Cincinnati, they offered to send an engine for her, if she was willing to ride in the engineer's cab.

"This was the best arrangement that could be made, for it was Sunday. I had traveled on a locomotive before in emergencies, and so at one o'clock, dressed for the lecture, and wrapped from head to foot as a protection from dust and cinders, I started with the engineer. We spun along merrily until within sixteen miles of our destination, and then came upon a derailed freight train. We could go no farther. Consulting various time tables that hung in the cab, the engineer's face suddenly brightened. 'In seven minutes,' said he, 'a fast cattle train leaves the next station beyond the broken down freight, which goes through to Cincinnati without stopping. We must catch that train Madam.'

"He assisted me to alight, and then to mount into a beer wagon which some one had hitched to a post, climbed in himself, and drove rapidly. There was no seat for me, so I stood behind the driver and steadied myself with my hands on his shoulders, not a little concerned about my feet, over which the empty beer kegs in the bottom of the wagon were in danger of rolling."

MY RIDE IN A BEER WAGON.

--From *The Story of My Life*

I AM BILLED AS "LIVE STOCK."

-- From *The Story of My Life*

They arrived just as the cattle train was about to leave and, although the crew first balked at the idea, she persuaded the trainmen that she was, indeed, livestock and they took her into the city riding in the caboose, not the cattle car. Once there they asked her to step on a scale and, "The bill was made out according to my weight avoirdupois, and I did what my four footed traveling companions never do -- I paid my bill and took a receipt for it."

A Grand Rapids paper reprinted an account from the *Cincinnati Gazette* that the audience "waited patiently an hour and a quarter for her arrival."

Her autobiography goes on to relate tales of being snowbound in Iowa, being delayed by wrecked trains in upper Michigan, crossing the Missouri River on a storm-tossed ferry boat which caught fire in mid-stream, and discovering a party of men in her hotel room. She shrugged them all off as hardships that a traveling lecturer must endure.

Hardships to be endured did not include, apparently, a six-mile journey by open carriage on a fine January day in western Michigan.

Mrs. Mary A. Livermore at 70.

GEORGE W. MAHER
Prairie on the Lakeshore

George W. Maher, Chicago architect, began his summer visits to the lakeshore before 1900, and by 1910 the family had a going fruit farm and a little enclave of cottages near 126th Avenue, at least two reflecting the Prairie-style architecture espoused by Maher and many of his Chicago colleagues including Frank Lloyd Wright and George Elmslie.

George Washington Maher was born in 1864 in Mill Creek, West Virginia, where his father was serving as a recruiting officer for the Union army. He was apprenticed as a teenager to Chicago architects Augustus Bauer and Henry Hill, and in 1887, went to work as a draftsman for another Chicago architect, Joseph Silsbee. That same year Silsbee had signed on another young draftsman, Frank Lloyd Wright, who noted in his autobiography that Maher's wages were $18 a week, compared to his own $12 a week. Wright, not known for his modesty, wrote, "I soon found George no better draughtsman than I was, if as good." George Grant Elmslie was also a co-worker.

The Prairie Style of architecture, which emphasized horizontal lines, earth tones and organic design motifs, was a movement that began about 1897. The style was called Prairie after the Illinois "prairie" or grassland. Actually most of the houses built in that style were constructed in wooded suburbs.

Maher took the organic ideas of the Prairie style and went one step further with his motif-rhythm theory. He wrote in 1907 that his fundamental principle was "to receive the dominant inspiration from the patron, taking into strict account his needs, his temperament, and environment, influenced by local color and atmosphere in surrounding flora and nature. With these vital impressions at hand, the design naturally crystallized and motifs appear which being consistently utilized will make each object, whether it be of construction, furniture or decoration, related."

George W. Maher

Employing the motif-rhythm theory he designed structures using as a decorative motif the poppy, lily, thistle, hollyhocks, and, in the case of one of the Lake Michigan cottages, the lake and dunes. Like many of his architect colleagues, when possible he preferred to design not only the building, but the stained glass windows, furniture, lamps, fountains, decorative urns, fencing, and occasionally the landscaping plan, so that all might be part of a coherent whole.

In 1893 Maher was married to Elizabeth Brooks, a talented water color painter. George and Elizabeth (Brooks) Maher and their son Philip, who had been born in 1894, and her parents, Alden and Ellen (Woodworth) Brooks, came to the lakeshore south of Saugatuck before 1900, landing by boat at Pier Cove. Alden Brooks was a Chicago portrait painter, and he may have heard of the area from a number of Chicago artists who painted in Saugatuck in the summers as early as the 1880's. Some of these artists became the founders of the Ox-Bow Summer School of Painting in 1910, and a note found among family papers indicates that Brooks participated in classes there. George Maher was also acquainted, certainly by 1904, with architect Thomas Eddy Tallmadge, an Ox-Bow founder, and a fellow member of the Chicago Architectural Club, which met in the club rooms of the Art Institute of Chicago. Tallmadge was also a writer and is credited with coining the phrase, "Chicago School" to describe the work of Maher and his contemporaries.

In the earliest days the Maher and Brooks party stayed at Weed's Resort, called Fernwood, in the southwestern corner of Saugatuck Township. The resort was operated by George E. Weed, son of Joshua Weed who had come to the lakeshore in 1833. Joshua was a carpenter by trade who built many of the earliest buildings in that area including the first Methodist church at Pier Cove. He was also one of the founders of the Douglas Basket Factory. When he died in 1901 at the age of 84, his sons George and Perry, inherited portions of the homestead. George was an active fruit farmer, ran Fernwood, and fished commercially. Perry was an accomplished violinist and studied and performed for many years in Europe, mostly Germany. After his return to his Saugatuck-area farm he spent a great deal of time in Chicago where he performed and taught violin. Later he gave up the farm and moved to Holland as a violin teacher. The third Weed son was Elmer E., who inherited his father's interest in the basket factory and would later become a moving force in Saugatuck's Big Pavilion.

Fernwood, in the early days of the twentieth century, was

more like a farmhouse than a resort. A large living room and parlor were reserved for the use of the guests. Meals were served in a very large dining room. The 17 guest rooms shared a single bath, and a three-holer with polished wood seats was located out near the barn. Whitefish, a staple on the Fernwood menu, was supplied from their own commercial fishing operation. Chase Creek runs through Weed Ravine and exits into Lake Michigan on the property. There was a fish house for the cleaning and processing of fish near the mouth of the creek, and a net-tending boat which was run up on the beach. The Weeds also owned their own pile driver, a scow-like vessel used to drive piling into the floor of Lake Michigan to hold the large nets used to catch fish. The nets were emptied daily and yielded, in addition to whitefish, some trout and an occasional sturgeon. Peach and cherry orchards ran from Lakeshore Drive to the Blue Star Highway, the rows of trees sometimes stretching 1800 feet.

Probably before 1906 the Mahers and the Brooks families purchased their own land in section 32 of Saugatuck Township just north of the Weed property. They camped in tents on their new property before permanent buildings were constructed. For several years after the construction of permanent buildings a wooden floor remained in the woods that had been used as the base for the tent. Lakeshore Drive was then located twenty to 50 feet west of its present location, and 126th Avenue is remembered as a sand trail through the woods. "The ruts were so deep that once you got the wagon started, you didn't have to guide the horses," a nephew recalls.

About 1908 Maher built a home at what later was designated 2582 Lake Shore Drive. In its original form "the bungalow" exhibited the horizontal lines and organic overtones of the Prairie style. The building was on the lake side of the road, with a tennis court between the house and the road. When it was first built there was a considerable expanse of lawn between the building and the shoreline, but erosion annually took a chunk of the ground. George Maher was concerned about the shrinking lot and attempted to alleviate the problem by digging parallel to the bank, and installing drain tile between the layers of soil. After his death erosion threatened the supports for the porch and the entire structure had to be moved back. Later the crumbling Lake Michigan shoreline again threatened and the building was moved a second time and is now located about where the tennis court once stood.

George Maher's bungalow before the 1922 remodeling. This painting is by Elizabeth (Brooks) Maher.

The house, as originally designed, had a living-dining room which bisected the long side of the rectangle. Bedrooms were located to the south, the kitchen and another bedroom to the north. There was a large screened porch on the south end, and a narrower porch on the lake side. About 1922 additional rooms were added to the north. The brick fireplace in the living room had an inscription above:

**Light your fires and never fear,
Life was made for love and cheer.**

Not long after the bungalow was constructed Alden and Ellen Brooks built a small cottage to the south. This cottage was located at 2578 Lakeshore Drive and was occupied by various members of the family until the 1920's. It was a one bedroom cottage, with a cot in one end of the living area for visiting grandchildren. The motto over this fireplace said :

The Time to be happy is now;
The Place to be happy is here.

In addition to Elizabeth (called Bessie) who married George Maher, there were two other Brooks daughters, Frances (called Fanny) Wyld, and Carol (called Carrie), and a son Merle, who died young. Fanny's daughter, Violet, lived with the Mahers most of her life after the age of 10. Ellen Brooks kept summer diaries of family activities and events, "It has been a perfect day, the lake is dashing its waves on the beach, the moon is just rising from behind the tree, and the voices of the revelers returning from the dance reminds me that the hour is late. It is a happy night scene."

Landis Lodge

The third building in the complex was Landis Lodge constructed about 1910 on the east side of Lakeshore Drive just south of 126th Avenue, for George's widowed sister, Mary (Maher) Hooker. Although there is some Tudor influence evident in the design of the cottage it also reflects the Prairie school with geometric masses, horizontal lines, and earth tones. For the two-story living room area Maher designed a large square stained-glass chandelier with blue and gold-colored glass that repeats the textures and colors in the dunes and lake outside. Fireplace andirons carry a swirling waves motif. Over the brick fireplace Alden Brooks painted a couplet:

**A summer well spent
Brings a year of content.**

The three buildings were usually referred to as "the bungalow, the cottage, and the lodge." There was also an old stucco farm house south of the cottage which served as living quarters for local farmers who were hired to oversee the Maher orchards and gardens, and farm buildings down a long driveway east of Lakeshore Drive near the farmhouse. The entire complex was called Hilaire, a family name, the middle name of George's grandfather. It had been suggested by his father as a name for the house in Kenilworth, Illinois, but he chose to use it in Michigan instead.

The Maher property holdings were extensive. A 1913 plat map shows one plot of 46.25 acres labeled G. W. Maher, another plot to the north of 48.00 acres labeled G. H. Mayer (apparently an error on the part of the cartographer since this is the lot where the bungalow was located), and a very thin 10 acre plot running from the lake along the south side of 126th Avenue labeled Mary Hooker.

Hilaire was a successful fruit farm. An early worker was Duff DuShane who came in 1911. Beginning in the fall of 1913 until about 1921 Logan Bartholome was in charge, and later Floyd Lamoreux. The newest scientific methods of farming were used. Produce included peaches, Greening apples, two varieties of pears, cherries and a small grape vineyard. At one time there was also a green bean field east of the road. Maher had a modern barn, with cement floor, a box stall, and feed chutes coming down from the loft. The packing house was large and had double doors on both sides so a wagon could be driven through, unloaded, and could continue out the other side. There was also a two story chicken coop. During World War I Maher purchased a fruit dryer with the idea that he would be able to send dried fruit to the troops, but it was never used. Most of the fruit was sold through the Saugatuck Fruit Exchange. Hilaire owned one of the first trucks to be used in the area, a Model T Ford. Because of the excellence of the fruit produced, commissionmen from Chicago would sometimes ask to tour the facilities, according to a Bartholome son. In addition to the orchards the resident farmer planted and tended a vegetable garden south of the house, which supplied the families with fresh produce.

They kept a cow for fresh milk, delivered daily by one of the Bartholome boys. After their old faithful Pansy died, Bessie Maher set out to obtain another cow. Her mother recorded in June of 1916: "The beautiful Jersey cow that Bessie chose of Mr. Atwater's dairy proves a very jewel for cream and milk and is a precious specimen of bovine beauty, they all say." There were also Gyp and Gill, the farmhorses, and Prince, the carriage horse, "The faithful farm horses are too full of business to be driven for pleasure," Mrs. Brooks explained. When the Bartholome family moved into the farmhouse there was a bonus, "Little Mrs. Bartholome flits back and forth like a little brown sparrow, so cheery and happy. She bakes our bread, which is delicious." The Mahers usually also brought their maid Tillie, who did most of the cooking at the bungalow.

Other neighbors were Jervis and Jane (Updyke) Kibby to the north, and William and Alice (Squier) Kibby to the east. The Jervis Kibbys were owners and hosts at the Douglas House in Douglas from 1874 to 1910, when they sold the hotel and retired to a house on 68th Street, and several fruit farms in the area. The William Kibby family began fruit farming along the lakeshore as early as 1870 and were especially noted for their strawberry crop. A son, Claude, sailed on the Great Lakes and was lost September 9, 1929, in the sinking of the ore carrier *Andaste* in Lake Michigan between Holland and Saugatuck.

Rev. George Horswell, pastor of the Kenilworth Union Church, the family church back in Illinois, owned a cottage and property to the north. It is not known whether he began coming to the area before, or after, the Mahers and Brooks.

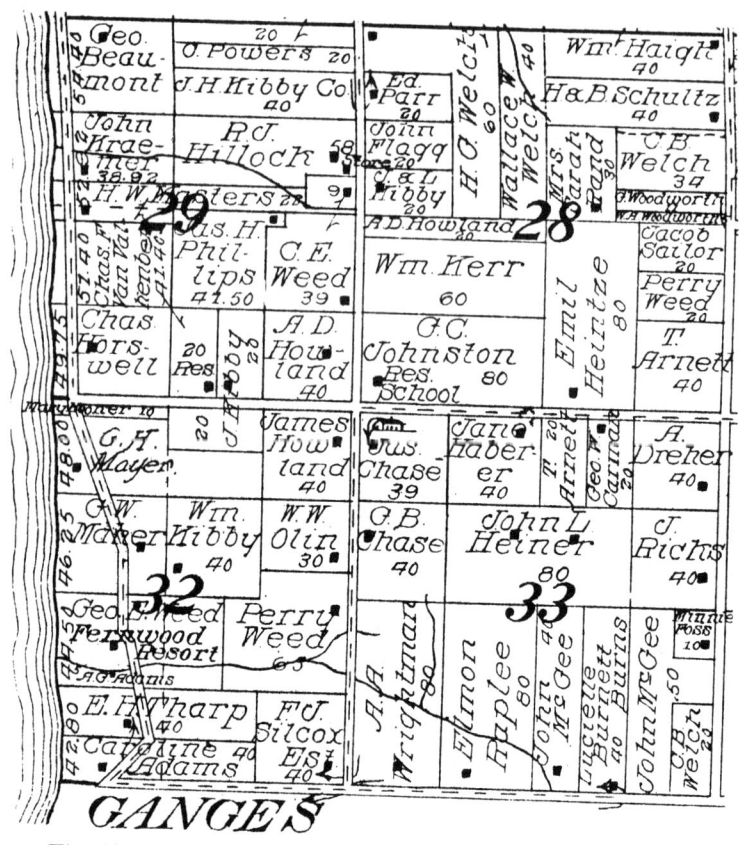

The 1913 atlas map showing Fernwood, lower left, and the Maher property, center. 126th Avenue bisects this map.

George Maher was interested in automobiles and bought a vehicle during a trip to Paris, which he had shipped to the United States. By the time the boats stopped running to Pier Cove the Maher and Brooks families could drive to their cottages on Lakeshore Drive. Another alternative was to put the car on a boat in Chicago, unload it at the dock in Holland, and drive it down.

Maher continued to design homes and commercial buildings. The Chicago suburbs of Kenilworth, Evanston, Oak Park, Highland Park, and Winnetka, are especially rich in Maher designs. He also created buildings in Wausau, Wisconsin, and designed Swift Hall, and the Patten Gymnasium on the campus of Northwestern University, in Evanston, Illinois.

A later writer, in attempting to assess the relative contributions of members of the Chicago School, wrote: "Maher cannot be dismissed lightly. His influence on the Midwest was profound and prolonged and, in its time, was certainly as great as was Wright's... His work showed considerable freedom and originality and his interiors were notable for the open and flowing space. His designs were easily emulated, they also embodied the ideals cherished by the client."

In addition to the three cottages in the Maher compound on the lakeshore, Maher left other marks on Saugatuck. In 1923, during what one architectural writer has termed his "Colonial Revivalism Lapse" he designed a columned colonial front for the Maplewood Hotel on Butler Street. The colonial designs that Maher did elsewhere are on buildings of unusually large scale. The Maplewood Hotel front is only massive by Saugatuck standards.

The building was constructed about 1865 as a home, furniture store, and undertaking parlor. In 1905 it was remodeled into a hotel by E.S. Pride and, in 1923, under new owners Frank and Carrie Wicks, became a "grand" hotel. "The front, quaintly beautiful, suggests a picture from an old book," the *Commercial Record* rhapsodized.

Members of the Wicks family are uncertain how Frank Wicks came to know George Maher, or how the novice hotel owner could finance the services of such as esteemed architect. "Dad drove a taxi for many years," a Wicks step-daughter said, "he knew practically everybody." She did remember meeting the two daughters of Mary (Maher) Hooker, Margaret (Janata) and Florence (Watts). During the remodeling Frank Wicks was seriously injured in a traffic accident and directed most of the work from a wheelchair. Despite rumors that would connect the Maplewood columns with a hotel at Singapore, or at early Port Sheldon, it is the recollection of the family that the 25-foot columns were new when installed. Many townspeople gathered when the large columns were delivered and hoisted into place.

The Maplewood Hotel shortly after the remodeling

Frank Wicks was president of the Village of Saugatuck in the 1950's, and it is through his efforts that a park was established on the riverfront. During the Bicentennial Celebration in 1976 this park was officially named for him. After selling the Maplewood in 1940 he and Carrie built Wickwood, a large dwelling and guesthouse on Butler Street north of the Maplewood Hotel. Lynn McCray, Saugatuck Village president 1961-70 was a later owner of the Maplewood Hotel. For many years the Saugatuck bus station was operated from a small office on the north side of the building. In 1991 the Maplewood Hotel, the front only slightly changed, was open as a bed and breakfast. Wickwood also was remodeled as a bed and breakfast in the 1980's.

After World War I Maher worked in community planning and did master plan work for Kenilworth, Glencoe, and Hinsdale, Illinois, and Gary, Indiana. In a 1923 issue of *American Architect* he urged architects to accept more responsibility for city planning.

Extending his concerns to smaller towns Maher spoke at a meeting in the spring of 1923 in the customers' rooms at the Fruit Growers State Bank in Saugatuck on the importance of planning and zoning. The newspaper reported, "Mr. Maher has been engaged in town planning and zoning work for several Illinois towns, and speaks from experience as to the benefits to be derived. His talk was in the nature of suggesting general outlines of a plan of which the details were to be taken up later. It is generally agreed that some movement along the line indicated by Mr. Maher should be instituted here, the only question being as to the scope feasible and practical under local conditions and environment." No official action was taken at that time, but the awareness of the need may have provided the impetus for the first Saugatuck plan approved after World War II and revised several times.

As early as 1890 Maher had suffered from depression. In 1925 the problem recurred and he was confined for about a year to a mental hospital in Wisconsin. After his release he came to Michigan to spend some time at Hilaire with a male attendant and several family members. Early Sunday morning, September 12, 1926, the family was unable to locate him, and roused residents in all the buildings in Hilaire. It was Violet Wyld and her brother, Merle, who found him dead in his car in the garage of the bungalow. He had shot himself in the head, first carefully rolling down the opposite window of the car, apparently to avoid breaking the glass with the bullet.

The *Commercial Record*, under the headline: "George Maher Shoots Himself," noted: "The community was greatly shocked by the tragic death of George Maher who shot himself in his garage at this summer home Hill-aire on the lakeshore early Sunday morning. . . Mr. Maher, for more than twenty years, owned the farm and summer home on the lakeshore and was highly respected by everyone who knew him."

Craig McLean, an admirer of Maher, and formerly editor of *Inland Architect*, sadly attributed his death to "a too constant strain upon a sensitive nature, and the demands made upon a none-too-robust constitution."

In 1985 the 75th birthday of Landis Lodge was celebrated. The cottage remains in the family.

CARL SANDBURG
Guest Lecturer

Around the turn of the century, culture and learning were in vogue and towns vied with each other to put together lecture programs for the entertainment and education of the people.

In the fall of 1908 Douglas, across the river from Saugatuck, had only recently expanded its school to full high school status, and had begun their own lecture series, to rival similar programs being offered in Saugatuck. A second series may also have been offered concurrently in Douglas by the Douglas Culture Club.

The December 11, 1908, *Commercial Record* carried the notice, under the Douglas Locals column:

"The third number of the lecture course will come Wednesday evening December 16. Chas. Sanburg will give a lecture entitled, 'The Mob and Civilization.' Mr. Jewell is of the opinion that the lecture will be one of the best things in the line we have ever had in Douglas."

The first lecture in the series had been Dr. J. A. Cousin speaking on "Tuberculosis and Open Air Treatment," in October. The November lecture was entitled, "The Spade and the Book, Our Thoughts of What Geology Has Done for the Bible," by Dr. Puffer.

Although the future author, biographer and poet was born Carl August Sandberg in his early years he took to using the first name Charles, and changed Sandberg to Sandburg. Dropping the d in the middle was probably an error on the part of the local type compositor. His name was printed as Charles

A. Sandburg on his first volume of poetry which had been published in 1904, a slim book of 39 buff-colored pages bound with a red ribbon entitled *In Reckless Ecstasy*. Two other small volumes followed in 1905, *The Plaint of a Rose* and *Incidentals*. It was his wife who preferred the more masculine Carl to Charles, and, after his marriage, the change was gradual. (He did her a similar service, and, although her family called her Lilian, Carl called her Paula, a name derived from Paus'l, a Luxembourg diminuitive used for young girls.)

In December of 1908 Carl was a thirty-year-old newlywed, living in Appleton, Wisconsin, where both he and his wife (sister of the famous photographer, Edward Steichen) were active in the Social Democratic Party, a forerunner of the Socialist Party. The party was politically strong in Wisconsin and Sandburg supported its philosophy of a better life for the average man. He had campaigned vigorously aboard the Red Special for Eugene V. Debs in the presidential election of 1908 and stayed on to work for the party in its Wisconsin office planning meetings, arranging for the distribution of party literature and helping the organization gain new members. He also made speeches on behalf of the party, and others that, although not officially party-sponsored, expounded the Social Democratic philosophy.

A letter written in 1908 by Sandburg from Appleton, to Reuben W. Borough In Marshall, Michigan, (whom he addresses as 'old Pal') states:

"I am dated for Medina on December 14 and Douglas, Michigan on December 16. Medina I have found on the map -- over near Toledo. Douglas I am not sure about - I suppose it is the one over in Allegan County near Grand Haven. Another date may be arranged for me -- tho this is not probable. Looking over the map (I have not made my route nor looked up time tables yet) it seems as though I will pass through or near Marshall. I shall make an attempt at stopping off at Jackson and seeing one Elmer Marshall there, who booked me these dates..."

THE world goes forward by personalities.

A suit of clothes can't talk with you nor shake hands nor touch your heart into new beauty and joy and knowledge. But what touching, tangible, beautiful things have been done by suits of clothes with men inside!

Books are but empty nothings compared with living, pulsing men and women. Life is stranger and greater than anything ever written about it.

CHARLES SANDBURG
LECTURER : ORATOR

Address care of THE LYCEUMITE,
Steinway Hall,
Chicago, Illinois.

A 1906 brochure advertising lectures by Charles Sandburg

Borough was a former reporter for the Ft. Wayne, Indiana, *Journal-Gazette*, and a fellow contributor to the poet journal *To-Morrow*. By 1908 he had returned to his hometown of Marshall, Michigan, to work for his father, a buggy manufacturer. He left for California in 1913. There is also some evidence in other correspondence that Sandburg had visited southwestern Michigan before stopping at Spring Lake, near Grand Haven.

According to a Sandburg biography most of the speeches of this era were strong political reading, based on increasing the rights of workers. The lecture, "The Civilization and the Mob," had been written in 1907 with some material salvaged from an earlier talk, "The Mob." A sample paragraph: "Labor is beginning to realize its power. We no longer beg, we demand old-age pensions; we demand a minimum wage; we demand industrial accident insurance; we demand unemployment insurance, and we demand the eight hour day which must become the basic law of the land."

In addition to the fee for the lecture, Sandburg also gained income from the sale of a recently published pamphlet, "You and Your Job," espousing the Socialist view of labor.

As the *Commercial Record* announcement testifies he was expected to address the audience in Douglas and there is no reason to believe that he did not. However no mention of the lecture is found in later editions of the local newspaper, and no further correspondence has been located that mentions the engagement.

The back files of the *Allegan Gazette* offer another interesting possibility. The December 19, 1908, issue of that paper, under the Saugatuck News heading carries the paragraph: "The third number of the lecture course at Douglas High School was not very well attended on account of the weather. The subject was 'The Poet of Democracy' by Walter Whitman. There will be two more of these lectures."

In May of 1908 Sandburg had addressed the literary society

of Appleton, delivering a speech on Walt Whitman called "The Poet of Democracy." This talk had replaced his very first publicly presented lecture which was entitled, "Walt Whitman; An American Vagabond." Whitman was one of his earliest poetic influences and Sandburg later wrote: "Walt Whitman took the word democracy and threw it around like a juggler does a fireball and wrestled it until it came to have something of the elements found in men's hearts and in the Gettysburg Address that made people understand the implications -- that whenever men have freedom there have been men who fought for it and died for it."

It is clear from the wording of the item in the *Journal* that the reporter had not attended the lecture, but was passing on news given him by others. He apparently wrongly understood that Walter Whitman was the speaker, rather than the subject. The speech that was not well attended because of the weather was probably Carl Sandburg's scheduled lecture. It is not known whether the subject of the lecture was reported incorrectly in the first place, or whether the speaker, faced with a small crowd which may have been more interested in poetry than political doctrine, changed his subject on the spot.

To get from near Toledo to Douglas with one day's travel time would have been at least an all night ride but might have been accomplished by taking a train to Chicago or perhaps South Bend, Indiana, then north to Holland. Or, if he had followed up on his plans to stop at Jackson or Marshall that he had written in his letter to Borough, he might have taken the train from Toledo to Detroit, then west to Kalamazoo, changing trains there for Grand Rapids. Both routes would have been completed by taking the interurban from Holland down to Saugatuck, thence by carriage (or foot) to Douglas.

Carl Sandburg was acquainted with the Saugatuck area, at least by name. In February of 1908, when he and his future wife were courting by mail, he sent her a trio of poems called "An Autumn Handful," which, because of the seasonal title, had probably been written some time previously. One of the three poems was called "Perspectives," and carries the parenthetical subtitle, "Inscribed to Saugatuck." The main title apparently takes note of the geographical fact that Saugatuck in Michigan, lies almost directly across Lake Michigan from Sandburg's point of view in Milwaukee, Wisconsin. In the poem he speaks of "the somber woodland" and "cool deep places" on the farther shore, with the broad blue vista of the lake in between.

After he became a recognized poet and writer, Carl Sandburg and his family lived in Michigan on a hill overlooking Lake Michigan at Harbert, near Benton Harbor, from 1926 to 1945, before they moved to a home in North Carolina to escape the winter winds. It was here the poet died in 1967.

* * * * * * * * * * * *

GOV. FRED M. WARNER

In July of 1908, Michigan Governor Fred M. Warner and Lieutenant Governor Patrick B. Kelley, accompanied by Congressman Gerrit J. Diekema and President Gerrit John Kollen of Hope College, paid a pre-campaign visit to Saugatuck. The July 17, 1908, *Commercial Record* reported:

"They came down from Holland on a special car and met a small crowd of citizens which gradually increased in size as the speakers proceeded with their talks from Seaton Arend's dray wagon which was backed up to the corner near the T.W. Leland residence on Butler Street. As the horses gave a start while Mr. Kelley was speaking the orator remarked that some politicians could not stand on their own platforms, but he believed, with the exercise of some gymnastics, he could do it."

* * * * * * * * * * *

D. K. LUDWIG
The Popcorn Millionaire

Selling popcorn at Saugatuck's Big Pavilion, about 1910, was the first commercial success of Daniel Keith Ludwig, and might be counted the foundation of his fortune which moved him to the top of the list as "the richest man in the world" in 1976.

That year John Paul Getty and Howard Hughes both died and the Sunday *Telegraph* of London, after an evaluation of the fortunes remaining, concluded that "the man upon whose elderly and seemingly reluctant shoulders the mantle of Richest Man in the World must fall is the almost completely unknown American tycoon, Daniel K. Ludwig."

Keith (in Michigan he was always called by his middle name) was born in South Haven, June 24, 1897, the son of Daniel Frank and Flora B. Ludwig. His father came from a family that had both a merchant and maritime tradition.

The patriarch of the clan, Keith's great-grandfather, Charles P. Ludwig, originally a blacksmith by trade, had built a commercial pier south of South Haven for the loading of lumber about 1870 and was also owner of the *Mary Ludwig*, an 85-foot lumber schooner launched in 1873, named for his wife. (Another schooner, the 58-foot long *Condor*, was owned by various members of the Ludwig family for many years. After it passed out of Ludwig hands it was damaged by ice April 1, 1904 in the Kalamazoo River near the old mouth at Fishtown, an enclave of fishermen's homes near the old lighthouse. Attempts to salvage the boat were unsuccessful and she lay for many years an often photographed and painted wreck. Eventually the battered hull sank and still lies under the waters of the Oxbow Lagoon. Most items of value have been removed by a century of divers and donated to various area museums.)

C. P. Sr. and Mary had 13 children. Nine boys (John, Charles Jr., Samuel, Franklin, Daniel, Lancaster, Van Beethoven, Herman, and William) and one girl (Mary) grew to maturity. The oldest were born in Pennsylvania; the others in Michigan where the family lived first in St. Joseph County, then about 1869 moved to South Haven Township, Van Buren County. The elder Ludwig ran a number of retail businesses at various times including a furniture store and a music store. As part of the music promotion each of the sons learned to play an instrument, and the nine formed a brass band that gave concerts.

Keith's grandfather, John Ludwig, the oldest son of C.P. and Mary, put his musical education to good service in 1861 when he enlisted at the age of 19 in the 11th Infantry Regiment as part of the band. About the time John's three year enlistment was up his next younger brother, C. P. Jr., turned 19 and enlisted in the same company as a bugler. Both boys returned to Michigan safely following the Civil War. In 1873 feeling the money pinch of a "financial panic," C.P. and Mary Ludwig, and at least the younger children, moved to a large farm near Saginaw. However, many of the older sons were sailors by trade, and several remained in, or returned to, west Michigan ports.

John married a woman named Julia, three years his senior. They had two children, Keith's father, Daniel Franklin, was born in 1873, and named for two of his uncles, Daniel, who was captain of the *Mary Ludwig* for several years, the youngest Master on the Great Lakes, and Franklin, also a sailor. Four years later a daughter, Nellie, was born. By the 1880 census, however, the couple was divorced. Julia was living with seven-year-old Frank, and three-year-old Nellie in South Haven Township where her occupation was listed as "keeps boarding house." It is likely that this is the old house near Ludwig pier. The elder Ludwigs retained ownership of the house and some land in South Haven Township, although at this time they were living in Saginaw. John, whose occupation was listed as sailor, lived in the Village of South Haven with two of his brothers.

Julia and Nellie left South Haven in 1889, settling eventually in Memphis, Tennessee. Frank did not see his mother or sister again until 1908. He seems to have remained in South Haven, living perhaps with his father, who eventually married again, or more likely with his grandparents who had returned to the area. When C.P. Sr. died in 1907, Frank was the only grandson chosen as a pallbearer. In 1894 Frank, then just over 21, was married to Flora, who was only 14. An 1898 directory of South Haven, published the year after Keith was born, shows Frank's occupation as sailor.

The family moved to Saugatuck in May of 1905 and rented a large white house on the hill on Hoffman Street near the Congregational Church. The home had formerly occupied by the Francis family. Keith's father was usually called "Lud" in Saugatuck, although most of the family addressed him as "Frank." He ran a real estate office, and was secretary and investor in the Big Pavilion, along with H. H. Engle and David Reid of South Haven, and E. E. Weed of the basket factory in Douglas. The building of the vast dance hall on the shores of the Kalamazoo River was announced in 1905, and it could be that the purpose of the Ludwig family's move to Saugatuck was to oversee its construction. The project met with several delays and was not actually begun until 1909.

There was also a family connection in Saugatuck. C.P. Ludwig Jr. had owned a lumber yard on the shores of the Kalamazoo River, located about where the Big Pavilion was later built. It is possible that nephew Frank had some hand in obtaining the property for the project. During his stay in Saugatuck, C. P. was also the leader of the local brass band. After the land was sold in 1905, he left for Holland and ran a hotel for a short time, before moving to Otsego where he opened a grocery store. Olive, a daughter of C.P. and cousin to Frank, was married in 1910 to Ira Koning, who, with his brother, took over the hardware store in Saugatuck that his father, John Koning, had begun before 1860.

Keith had attended the old Deerlick School in South Haven, for a brief time before the move north. He continued his schooling at the old Saugatuck School on the hill, within walking distance of the Ludwig residence. He was an adequate, but not very enthusiastic student, according to his former teacher, Mrs. Carl Bird. He did occasionally make the perfect attendance lists printed monthly in the local newspaper.

The dance floor of the Big Pavilion

The family settled into life in Saugatuck. Keith's mother (in Saugatuck she was usually called Belle which was probably her middle name) was a frequent hostess of The Thimble Club (a ladies' sewing group), and a vocal soloist at many Saugatuck Woman's Club events. The newspaper social columns report that she participated in a program at the Woman's Club in April of 1906 and read a paper, "Poets Whose Poems Have Influenced National Affairs," and in 1907 "talked on the origins of 'Yankee Doodle.'"

A month after the move, the June 30, 1905, *Commercial Record* reported, "Keith Ludwig entertained a number of his playmates Monday afternoon at his home the occasion being his birthday. A delightful afternoon was spent in playing games and at 5 o'clock ice cream and cake was served."

The newpaper also reports frequent visits to friends and relatives in South Haven, and, less often, visitors in the Ludwig house from South Haven, most often the Hills, the family of Belle's sister. Shortly after the move Lud purchased an automobile "to use in connection with his real estate business." He made frequent business trips to Manistee, and in 1908 he opened a branch real estate office in Frankfort.

The Big Pavilion had been announced in 1905, but construction was not actually begun until the spring of 1909 when the enormous curved-roof wooden structure was completed in less than three months. The main floor was 200 x 100 feet and was built partially on pilings out over the river. Its curved arches, both inside and out, were lined with rows of electric lights powered by the Pavilion's own generator (electricity had not yet come to the village except for a few who were able to tap into the interurban lines). The best bands in the midwest were engaged to play for the dancing. Later a movie theatre was added, and, much later, a restaurant and bar. The entire complex burned to the ground in 1960.

Shortly after the building opened in 1909 Keith set up a shoeshine stand and, later, a popcorn concession. His next venture was an old boat he found down by the river which he refurbished and rented to vacationers. The boat eventually sold for twice the cost of his investment.

No one is quite certain if this is the same boat that he was working on when he approached a young friend in Douglas who was serving as an apprentice barber, with a business proposition that they go halves on a boat which he figured could be put into action for $35. The friend agreed and put $17.50 into the project. That fall, or the following year, Keith sold the boat and left town without repaying the $17.50 or sharing the profit. Schemes for collecting the monies due were a favorite topic at the barbershop in Douglas for many years.

Keith was one of "Whit's Boys," a group under the

leadership of Charles F. Whitcomb which formed what they called a YMCA with its headquarters at Whit's house on Holland Street. The group had a Christian emphasis, but also engaged in social activities and sports. One account claims that Keith always did display remarkable money know-how and was treasurer of their ball team. "He didn't play well," related a fellow team member, "but he knew how to get uniforms."

Other friends recall one Fourth of July that Keith and two friends were earning extra money setting pins at the old bowling alley on Water Street (the building was later the Old Rail Grill). He needed to go to the bathroom, but he did not want to give up his place. The end result was dampened pants and a good deal of ribbing from his friends.

Keith from a 1912 group shot of Whit's Boys.

Keith's father, was active in Saugatuck business affairs and a founder of the Saugatuck Businessman's Club, and later the Men's Club which had 37 members and their own clubhouse in downtown Saugatuck at the corner of Hoffman and Water Streets. The Men's Club was formed, according to a 1912 newspaper, as "a social club where members may pass spare time. There are card tables and facilities for other games of amusement." No gambling or liquor was allowed, however. In 1912 he contributed to a Saugatuck Boosting Fund which promoted the Saugatuck-Douglas area as a summer resort in newspaper advertisements in St. Louis, Chicago, Indianapolis, Cincinnati, Memphis and Kansas City. He also played second base on the East Side Saugatuck Businessmen's baseball team.

D. F. Ludwig
Real Estate
SAUGATUCK, - MICH.

Lud was a motivating force in the community. In 1906 he urged the community to stage a big celebration for Harbor Day, the day that a newly constructed mouth of the river would be dug through to Lake Michigan, and he was on the first boat to go through the new cut. In 1907 he secured permission from the Federal government to dam the upper end of Indian Cut, an attempt to reroute the Kalamazoo River a few miles east of town. In 1908 he circulated a paper to raise money to help support the Saugatuck Cornet Band, in July of that year he entered into negotiations with a company exploring the feasibility of building an electric railroad between Saugatuck and South Haven. In 1909, in addition to his responsibilities at the Big Pavilion, he started a subscription to secure money to rent and maintain a baseball grounds (and then was named manager of the grounds), and was successful in efforts to get an emergency appropriation to dredge the river near the dock of the *Aliber*, a passenger and fruit-carrying boat. It was in his downtown office window that unusual plants (for example, a four headed strawberry, an extra large ear of corn) were displayed, and where the plans for the Big Pavilion were available for inspection. He was also an active Republican and in 1911, according to the local newspaper, the caucus to elect delegates to the state convention was held at his office.

> REPUBLICAN TOWNSHIP CAUCUS
> A Repuplican township Caucus for the purpose of choosing eleven delegates to attend the County Convention to be held at Allegan on August 7, will be held at the office of D. F. Ludwig in the village of Saugatuck on Monday evening, August 5, at 8 o'clock.
> By order of Committee.

According to townspeople who knew the family, although Belle participated in some of the social activities of the town, she tended to dress a little bit fancier and gave the impression that the society of Saugatuck was a little too rustic for her liking. Lud is remembered as an outgoing likeable man, Belle as a little snobbish and standoffish. The couple had only one other child, born in 1898 apparently while they were still living in South Haven. The infant lived only 18 days.

Belle was very ill the spring of 1912, and by April was still not able to be out. In the August 23 issue of the *Commercial Record* was a paragraph: "D.F. Ludwig expects to take a trip down the Mississippi the coming winter, stopping at various places along the way to hunt. A month later was a note that, "B.E. Hyet expects to go south this fall to spend the winter. He will go by boat via the Mississippi River."

In October of 1912 the two parties set out separately and headed for Chicago. "Messrs. Hyet and Bierdsley left the forepart of this week for the South on the *Douglas*. They expect to spend the winter on the lower Mississippi." And in a separate paragraph, "D.F. Ludwig and family left the latter part of last week to spend the winter in the South. They went in their boat via the drainage canal and the Illinois River."

By October 25 the newspaper reported that they had reached Chicago, and in the November 15 issue the locals column noted: "D.F. Ludwig and Bert Hyet are almost to the Mississippi River on their way South. They have been getting plenty of game on the way and Bert Hyet expects to buy a load of apples to take south with him as he can get them for 15 cents a bushel where he is. Ed Gleason is not so far down the river as the others as he is trapping."

The trip does not sound like Belle's sort of journey, but on January 10, the newspaper notes: "Word is received from Mr. and Mrs. D.F. Ludwig in Mississippi State that they are enjoying themselves very much. They say the weather is fine." In April the *Commercial Record* carried a notice that "D.F. Ludwig likes the sunny south so well he has decided to remain there the coming season. "

Later the same month C. E. Bierdsley returned to Saugatuck to get his affairs in order for a permanent move and recounted that he and Bert Hyet on the *Douglas*, and D.F. Ludwig and family in their boat, had traveled together until they arrived at Baldwin, Louisiana where Hyet took a position in a machine shop. The others went on down the river to Port Arthur, Texas. The item concluded: "Mr. Ludwig is living in Port Arthur and using his boat as a ferry boat between that place and a nearby town. He likes the place very much and so does his family."

Bierdsley headed for Port Arthur in May with the intention of going into the boat business with D. F. Ludwig "as he owns an interest in the *Douglas* and Mr. Ludwig has a steady run for both boats."

The general impression has been in Saugatuck that D.F. Ludwig and son, Keith, left for the south without Belle. If the newspapers are to be believed she was along on the trip, or at least joined them at some point. However, in March of 1914 she was back in Saugatuck visiting friends and relatives, and left in mid April to spend the summer with her sister in Everett, Washington. The couple was eventually divorced, and Belle remained in Washington State, later moving to Seattle.

In February of 1916 Keith visited Saugatuck during a trip to Michigan. The news column in the local paper noted: "He still lives with his father at Port Arthur, Texas. His father owns a boat and makes a business of carrying fresh water from artesian wells up the river to Port Arthur where he supplies it to ocean going steamers. Keith works in a store." Lud's father, John, then 74 was also living in Port Arthur by 1916.

Keith was in the eighth grade when he left the old Saugatuck School on the hill. According to biographers that was the last of his formal schooling, except for classes to get his engineer's license. When he was 19 he left his job as a mechanic and borrowed $5,000, mostly on his father's signature, to buy a broken down old tanker. He got his money back selling the boat's unneeded equipment and rented the tanker to a dealer in molasses, a commodity much in demand because of its use in the production of alcoholic beverages. The U.S. was just beginning to feel the effects of nationwide prohibition.

He worked as a mechanic and engineer aboard a number of different kinds of vessels and at one point spent some time in Florida. One day his old teacher, Mrs. Carl Bird, received a crate-looking package in the mail. "My children were just little at the time," Mrs. Bird said later. "I got a hammer and started to open it and about that time some animal inside stuck his nose out through a hole in the boards, and I got out of there fast." Keith had sent her children a live alligator.

Lud remarried, another woman named Belle (or Isabelle), and the couple lived in Florida, near Bradenton. Occasionally they visited friends and relatives in Michigan.

Keith's fleet grew. After experiencing an explosion aboard one of his ships, during which rivets popped loose from the steel plates, he pioneered the use of welded seams. The shipping side of his fortune was founded on using surplus ships, mostly from the government. Deciding that oil was the cargo with the most profit, he began to specialize in tankers, purchasing and organizing refineries to supply the product. He later was one of the first shippers to use a supertanker. Ludwig built hotels in Bermuda, Grand Bahama Island, San Francisco, West Germany and Mexico. He became a land developer in several parts of the U.S. including Westlake Village in southern California, south Florida and New York, as well as the Bahamas and Australia. Other investments include salt evaporation fields, coal mines, potash fields and iron deposits in Canada, and savings and loan companies. His Anerican Hawaiian Company was one of the first to use container-carrying ships, with special dock facilities to enable trucks to simply drive the containers onto the ships, saving loading and unloading costs.

D. K. Ludwig in his fifties. Because of his camera shy ways this photograph has been used to illustrate magazine and newspaper articles about him for the last 40 years.

In 1967 he began work on his Jari project, in Brazil, a multi-million dollar dream which was designed to turn more than three million acres of jungle north of the Amazon River into an economically productive tree farm, rice paddy and cattle ranch. A woodburning power plant and a factory for producing cellulose from pulpwood were preassembled and floated from their assembly point in Japan around the southern tip of Africa and up the Amazon River where they were bolted to prepared foundations in a man-made lagoon. The project cost more than anticipated, and drew sharp criticism from some environmentalists. Many in the financial world credit the loss of capital on the Jari project with dropping Ludwig from the "richest man in the world" title, before 1980. His fortune, however, remains one of considerable proportions.

Keith married twice. His first wife was a show girl named Gladys whom he wed in Florida in 1928. She gave birth to a daughter in 1936. The couple was divorced in the spring of 1937. During his childhood in Saugatuck Keith had a serious illness, possibly the mumps, and at that time the doctors told his parents he would probably be incapable of having children in adulthood. This knowledge may have contributed to rumors that he feels it unlikely that the daughter is his biological child. Following the divorce he married a woman named Virginia (usually called Ginger). The couple lived in suburban Darien, Connecticut, and visited the local country club where Keith was seen often by former schoolmate Eileen (Kreager) DeBoer, daughter of Dr. H. E. Kreager who was president of the Village of Saugatuck, 1924-33. Never comfortable with being recognized he was not very friendly, she reports. In 1967 the Ludwigs donated their Darien house to a hospital and moved to downtown Manhattan. In 1991 they still occupy the penthouse of a 17-story co-op luxury apartment building which American-Hawaiian Steamship Co., a Ludwig company, had constructed in the 1960's at 5th Avenue and 60th Street, overlooking the southeast corner of New York's Central Park.

Efforts to contact Ludwig during the Saugatuck Centennial, and other hometown celebrations in the hope that he would return to Michigan to join in the festivities, or at least make a monetary contribution to the event, have not been successful. However, in 1978 a secretary did send for several copies of an article in the *Commercial Record*, that included a photograph of Whit's Boys with a 12-year old Keith Ludwig, nattily attired in overcoat and cap, lounging in one corner of a couch.

* * * * * * * * * *

MRS. JAY GOULD ?

"Saugatuck people as a rule are not aware that for a time this place was the residence of a woman who now claims to be able to prove that she was the first and only legal wife of Jay Gould.

"The woman in question resided here some 12 or 14 years ago, occupying the little cottage near the ferry where she passed by the name of Mrs. Youngpeter.

"The story as it is being told through the papers is that when this woman, whose maiden name was Sarah Ann Brown, was a girl of 15 years she visited relatives in New York, where she met and married Jay Gould, then a lad of 17 with neither money nor prospects.

"The young couple separated after a few months and Mrs. Gould returned to her former home where she resumed the name of Brown. A daughter was born to this union, however, Gould was never made aware until after the death of his second and acknowledged wife in 1880.

"The first Mrs. Gould would never consent to an effort to establish her claim and it was the daughter, Mary Ann Angell, who is now about to begin proceedings to prove herself the rightful heir to the Gould millions. She has near relatives living in both Saugatuck and Douglas."

--*Saugatuck Commercial*, October 12, 1894

[Jay Gould (1836-92) built an empire of railroads beginning about 1860. He also owned the *New York World*, the New York Elevated Railways and controlled Western Union Telegraph Co. He was considered one of the wealthiest men of his era. The suit mentioned above, if it was filed, cannot be traced.]

AMELIA EARHART
A Summer at Camp

In the summer of 1917 when she was 20 years old Amelia Earhart, later one of the first female airplane pilots, spent at least two weeks at Camp Gray on the shores of Lake Michigan, across the Kalamazoo River from the Village of Saugatuck.

She came to the camp near the end of July, at least partly to get out of Kansas City where her parents were having marital problems. During an earlier trial separation Amelia, her mother and sister, had lived with the Shedd family in Chicago. She had graduated from Hyde Park High School in Chicago in June of 1916 and had many friends in the city. The trip to Camp Gray was planned with a school friend named Sarah (sometimes called Cy).

Although she was 20 years old Amelia had spent most of her life within the confines of her family, or at boarding schools and she was surprisingly naive for her age. The summer of 1917 was important in her life primarily because it occasioned her first important social interaction with members of the opposite sex, an introduction she seemed to truly enjoy. At least some of the events of that summer are recorded in a series of letters she penned to her mother that have been preserved in the Arthur and Elizabeth Schlesinger Library on the History of Women in America, Radcliffe College, Cambridge, Massachusetts.

Two of the letters are written on Camp Gray stationery which is of two types, one has a printed "Camp Gray" at the top and includes the words: "A Delightful, Healthful Resort. A Miniature Range of Mountains Covered with a Beautiful Forest Fronting on Lake Michigan and Having a Rare Bathing Beach." Also "Selden C. Adams Superintendent" and "Dr. George W.

Gray Founder." The second includes a photograph of "George W. Gray DD Founder" and includes the words: "CAMP GRAY is situated in the outing park of the Forward Movement Association, which consists of a miniature range of mountains densely covered with forest and fronts on Lake Michigan. Its bathing beach is unsurpassed." One of the preserved envelopes bears a Saugatuck, Camp Gray Station, postmark.

Amelia Earhart in late 1917 or early 1918 after she had left school to become a volunteer nurse in Toronto.

The camp that would later be called Camp Gray was opened in 1899 by Rev. George W. Gray, Methodist pastor, educator, city missionary, and founder of the Forward Movement Association of Chicago. He sought a cool place for people from the city to come in the summertime. The first campers were children, and occasionally their mothers, escaping the heat of the city to spend a week or two in the Michigan woods. Later the program was expanded to girls and young women of the work force, as a cheap and safe alternative to more worldly resorts. Early in the history of the Forward Movement camp Rev. Gray instituted rental housing suitable for middle and upper class families of Chicago where, he said, "the working class could associate with people of means." Rev. Gray died in 1913, and in 1916 the name of the camp was changed to Camp Gray in his honor. The most prominent building of the early camp was Swift Villa, a large dining room and lodge complex, donated in 1899 by the widow of Gustavus Swift, of the Swift Meat Packing Co. of Chicago. (It was destroyed by fire in 1954.)

Swift Villa

Amelia's father had seen her by train at least part of the way to Chicago, and her first letter to her mother back in Kansas City notes, "Poppy was such a lamb last night I came near coming back with him."

The letter postmarked Chicago was mailed July 31, 1917, and begins: "I have been here for about forty-five minutes -- calling up Mr. Tredwell's home to find out whether Cy had gone (which she has) and checking my baggage and buying a ticket to Holland which is $3.91. Pete said Sarah left at six this morning. As we found I leave at noon. The trip here was lovely as far as service etc. was concerned but I never was on such a beastly dirty trip in my life. I scrubbed my face and neck so hard it looks as tho I had hives. . ."

On her arrival at the camp she must have received a letter from her mother that included the news that her mother had moved from the family home on Charlotte Street in Kansas City and was living at the Hotel Sutherland. Although she did not comment on the marital situation, all subsequent letters were addressed to her mother at the hotel. She also responded negatively to a suggestion that must also have been in the letter that her younger sister Muriel (sometimes called Pidge in the family) should join her at Camp Gray.

A Saugatuck, Camp Gray Station, postmark

Her response to her mother's letter reads in part: "I surely have had a wildly exciting time and don't send Pidge without wiring for accommodations as there is not a vacant place. I will see what I can do today. Mother, Sarah is not here yet! When in Chicago I called Pete and she said she had left at six o'clock. Well they just took off the day boats, the route she told Mrs. Merrill she intended to take and she evidently will get in this morning instead of last night as expected. However I arrived then and had a dreadful time finding my way. I thot ["thought", Amelia often wrote in a sort of shorthand] it most peculiar not to be met etc. and fortunately met the camp Major domo who escorted me over. Very thankful to be under his protection. Well, reached here and bumped (figuratively) into Mr. Merrill at the desk. He flew out and came back with Mrs. Merrill who was just lovely. We are in one of her rooms. Her daughter's, who is in Vermont, the only vacant room on the place. Ken is here and took me immediately to play in the sand and walk on the beach a delightful experience despite high heels. . . Things are rather primitive but the waitresses are all college girls working their way thru. I have just had breakfast and while not elegant very good for camp. We are all going over for Sarah so must end this to mail."

At this time there was no regularly scheduled service directly to Saugatuck and campers arriving by boat from Chicago landed in Holland. Here they either took the electric railroad the twelve miles south to Saugatuck, or were met by the camp wagon. The summer of 1917 was also about the time that Chicago campers began arriving by train at Fennville, a small farming community about six miles east of Saugatuck where the Pere Marquette Railroad trains picked up passengers and fruit. At Fennville the campers were met by a camp bus or truck. In subsequent years, as boat service became more uncertain, the majority of campers who did not arrive in family cars came by train. Later bus service was also used. Amelia indicates that she was fortunate to make an unplanned rendezvous with a camp staff member at the boat dock in Holland.

The Merrill family were apparently friends from Chicago, Ken Merrill was to be Amelia's favorite part of the camp experience. She wrote her mother on Camp Gray stationary at some point during her stay:

Bluebird Cottage at Camp Gray, about 1920.

". . . Under no circumstances could K. and Muriel come up without you. There is not a place and it is impossible to be alone. Sarah and I would be lost without the Merrills as Mrs. Merrill has been kindness itself and Ken has toted me around considerably. . .

"Things are very primitive and the food is not very good, however probably conducive to rugged health it may be, tho I have my doubts about the nutritive value of oleomargerine. The only desirable qualities are the climate and scenery and I am having a wonderful time just being with Sarah. I should never choose it as an ideal place without friends to make one overlook lack of hot water, oil lamps etc. . . ."

These were war years and some foodstuffs, including butter, were becoming expensive and hard to find which probably accounts for the use of oleomargarine. Municipal electric power had been established in Saugatuck in 1912, but apparently lines had not yet been run to bring the camp into the system.

The property of Camp Gray reached from the Kalamazoo River just south of the ferry landing, to Lake Michigan. During Amelia's stay there in 1917 there was considerable local controversy about attempts of the camp staff to keep outsiders from wandering about on camp property. The first accusation was that those using the Lincoln Road, a predecessor of the Oval Beach Road, were being halted and asked to secure a pass from camp headquarters. In the August 9, 1917, *Commercial Record* camp superintendent Selden C. Adams called the accusations untrue. "No one is ever interfered with who travels the Lincoln Road. This affords a direct path to and from the beach, over which the public has a perfect right to travel." He then explained that it was true that "persons other than our guests" who wanted to enter the camp grounds were being asked to apply for the privilege at the camp office. He concluded the letter, "The Forward Movement Association regrets that it has become necessary to restrict outsiders, but this action was forced by trespassers who take liberties which are not accorded even to our guests... Good citizens desiring to visit our grounds may do so by properly identifying themselves at our office."

After two weeks her Chicago friends left, and camp rapidly lost its luster for Amelia. She wrote her mother in a letter postmarked August 14, "Your selfish and guilty feeling daughter is coming home. I can't stand it any longer and especially as Sarah could, but does not feel as tho she ought to stay longer we will both leave tomorrow Wednesday the fifteenth. I have enough money to get to Chicago after paying board at only $9.00 per week and as Kenneth and Harry left day before yesterday and have planned opera and base ball games etc. for a few days I said I thot you would let me stay at Mr. Tredwell's after their strong invitation. The boys have been lovely and Kenneth has done so much for me. He is very nice and sensitive and almost brilliant. We four have just ideal times together and have gone on innumerable canoe trips, reading jaunts, etc. together. I can't think of hot weather since it is almost too chilly for comfort, but I can not bear to be so privileged. Mother may write to Mrs. Merrill if she feels it proper. She is a dear and has been so brave thru so many many trials. Her oldest son just now is awaiting a hoped for commission; her middle son is going and her daughter is very ill besides lots of other things..."

Missing from Amelia's synopsis of activities is any comment on the Village of Saugatuck with its Big Pavilion which would have been in full swing in August, the skating rink directly across the river from the Camp Gray canoe docks, and all of the other amusements offered by the summer resort community. Because Lake Michigan is usually too rough for small unstable boats, the camp canoes have always been kept at a small dock on the Kalamazoo River just to the south of the ferry. If Amelia and her friends went canoeing it would have been on the river and they would have paddled within sight of the pavilion and other amusements of the town. If they succumbed and went dancing or box bowling, she was apparently not eager to relate this to her mother.

Things did not work out in Chicago and she explained it all in a special delivery letter to her mother written the next day. The letter is postmarked August 16, 1917, and was apparently mailed by Sarah in Chicago on her return. It is not until the third page that Amelia mentions the real reason why another week or two at Camp Gray wouldn't be so bad after all.

"Received word last evening that Mrs. Tredwell was not well and was going to the hospital for a few days to take radium treatments. Mr. Tredwell urged me to come however if I would not mind being quiet but of course I declined and will stay here until I can come home as per my preceding letter...

"... I can stay here indefinitely except for the fact that Ken will come up to see me over the weekend and without Sarah I should not feel quite comfortable -- it seeming as tho I might possibly be waiting for him and doing it purposely. However if it is inconvenient to have me home I will gladly stay. There are several very nice girls of about fifteen or so and a small group of older women and one boy of twenty-three who is exceptionally fine and who has been very nice to me whenever he could. He is an old family friend of the Tredwells and he and his mother are here for a while longer. I like her so much. His father was on Roosevelt's personal Rough Rider staff and was very well known. Gordon Pollock is his name. He is very interested in photography and was offered a position as war photographer but refused it to go into the aviation corps. He has made several dozen studies of me which I am anxious to see and which I hope will be good. . . "

There is no further correspondence from Camp Gray and camp records do not exist for pre-1920 years so it is uncertain how much longer Amelia stayed in Michigan. She corresponded with Ken, Harry and Gordon for several years. In October Amelia returned to school at the Ogontz School, in Pennsylvania north of Philadelphia, but left after Christmas without graduation to work as a volunteer nurse's aide in Toronto to aid the war effort. She also became concerned about the diet offered the patients. It was during this time in Toronto that she had a life-changing experience with an "aeroplane". It was a small red stunt plane at the Toronto exposition which "said something to me as it swished by," she later wrote.

In the summer of 1920, after a short time at Columbia University where she determined that medicine was not her field, Amelia left for Los Angeles where her parents were trying once again to mend their marriage. (They were finally divorced in 1924.) In 1921 Amelia had her first flying lesson and bought her first airplane, a Kinner Canary. In 1928 she was the first woman to fly across the Atlantic (as a passenger), and in 1929 finished third in the First Women's Transcontinental Air Derby, later dubbed the first Powder Puff Derby.

In 1931 she was married To George Palmer Putnam, 12 years her senior, who had served as publicist for the trans Atlantic flight. The following year she became the first woman to fly the Atlantic solo, and the first woman to fly solo across the United States making the trip from Los Angeles to Newark in 19 hours, 14 minutes and 10 seconds.

On the first of June 1937, Amelia Earhart and Fred Noonan, navigator, left in a Lockheed Electra to circumnavigate the globe. The plane disappeared on July 2 enroute from Lae, New Guinea to Howland Island, a small island nearly astride the equator on a path halfway to Honolulu. Despite many books, magazines and newspaper stories which have speculated about the fate of the flight and intimated that the Electra was on a secret mission for the U.S. government, or that the Japanese, then preparing for what would become World War II, were in some way involved with her disappearance, the family, represented in 1990 by her sister Muriel (Earhart) Morrissey, feels with certainty that Amelia's plane got within 100 miles of Howland Island, and went down looking for the small island after 20 hours and 16 minutes of flight from New Guinea, and that her death was a tragedy of the sea.

Camp Gray was sold in 1921 to the Presbytery of Chicago which continued the summer camp for children, and gradually phased out the housekeeping cottages. The grounds were also used for meetings, and seminars. In 1940 the first Christian Ashram in the United States was held there under the leadership of E. Stanley Jones. In 1990 the ministry of the camp continues with an added emphasis on year-round camping of family and church groups. It is now known as Presbyterian Camps.

IGNACE JAN PADEREWSKI
Lakeshore Serenade

Oldtime residents and cottagers of the Douglas lakeshore relate stories of the day, or days, that noted Polish pianist Ignace Jan Paderewski played the piano while an appreciative audience gathered on the lawn outside to listen.

His hosts for the visit were John F. and Harriet (Mikitynski) Smulski of Chicago, who owned a large white and green summer home, at that time three buildings south of Center Street on Lakeshore Drive.

Paderewski, born in 1860 in the province of Podolia in Russian Poland, showed an early aptitude for music, which his father encouraged. He began his concert career in Vienna in 1887, and made the first of many American concert tours in 1891. Chicago was one of his favorite stops. He wrote later in his memoirs, "Chicago had impressed me more than any other city in America... when I first arrived in New York one of the largest buildings at that time was the Windsor Hotel. Chicago already had several skyscrapers." He gladly returned to Chicago in 1893 in conjunction with other events ocurring at the World's Fair, and he included the city in his itinerary whenever he was in the United States.

At the close of World War I, seeking to help unite the people of Poland, he became the first premier of the Republic of Poland, and also held the position of Minister of Foreign Affairs. After he resigned as premier he was sent as Poland's delegate to the League of Nations. Although his service in that office was of short duration, the title of Premier followed him for the rest of his life. Miriam (Caylor) McLaughlin, whose parents, Worth and Katherine (Vaughan) Caylor of Chicago, had the cottage north of the Smulskis, in relaying the stories of Paderewski's visit, noted that his hosts and other socially correct lakeshore visitors always referred to Paderewski as "the Premier."

Ignace Jan Paderewski

The cottage that the Smulskis occupied had been built about 1908 by Robert J. Moore, of the local Moore lumber family. After his departure it was owned by several summer residents from Chicago. The Smulski family purchased it about 1920. In 1926 it was enlarged and remodeled.

John F. Smulski was born in Poland, near Posen, in 1867. He came to Chicago with his family and worked in the family publishing business, chiefly Polish language publications. Beginning in 1898 he held a series of political offices, first as alderman for the 16th ward of Chicago, president of the West Park Commission, and two terms as state treasurer. In 1906 he founded the North Western Trust and Savings Bank, at Milwaukee and Division, Chicago. He had a special interest in helping new immigrant families from his native Poland invest wisely. Smulski, with Paderewski and Bishop Rhode headed the Polish National Committee *(Polski Wydzial Narodowy)* that co-ordinated Polish support activities in the United States during World War I. It was this committee that is credited with making it clear to U.S. President Woodrow Wilson that Paderewski spoke for Polish people everywhere when he pleaded the cause of Poland's independence in the closing days of World War I. Moved, President Wilson supported Polish independence in 1917.

It was the Smulskis' custom to come to Douglas before the season actually began. Some years they were here as early as mid-April, and often did not depart until October. After their natural-born children died as infants, the couple adopted twins in 1912. They were named after the parents, the boy was John Jr., sometimes called Jack, and the girl was named Harriet. When they were still in the primary grades they would enroll in the Douglas school after their arrival, until the end of the school year. The June 8, 1923, *Commercial Record*, records that at the school closing picnic at the County Park "which was enjoyed by parents as well as children, Mrs. John F. Smulski treated the school to ice cream." She also presented the school with a number of books. During most of this period the Douglas School, located on Center Street in downtown Douglas, went to the eighth grade, with high school students usually going on to Saugatuck as tuition students.

It is not certain what year Paderewski visited Douglas, but it would have to have been after the Smulskis purchased the cottage about 1920, and before 1928 when John Smulski died. According to oldtime lakeshore residents Paderewski was invited to the Smulski summer home on the lakeshore to give him a vacation. A piano, altered and tuned to his specifications, was shipped by rail to Fennville, then by truck to the cottage, so he could practice. Paderewski took his piano practice very seriously, and, according to his autobiography, felt that several hours of practice was absolutely essential before each concert performance even if the program was exactly the same as the program he had played the previous night.

Occasionally when he was in a city for a concert, he would be booked to play "at home" concerts for his hosts. Because this was to be his vacation the Smulskis did not ask the famous pianist to play a formal concert, but lakeshore residents passing by could hear him practicing. The Smulskis cooperated by leaving the windows and doors to the porch open. Lakeshore residents and their guests brought blankets and sat on the lawn to hear the music. To insure the Premier's privacy the event was not reported in the local newspapers.

The Smulski cottage on the Douglas lake shore.

Some oldtime lakeshore residents said they felt that Paderewski had visited more than once, but their recollections might be confused by memories of hearing beautiful piano music coming from the house on other occasions. Mrs. Smulski was an opera singer and an accomplished pianist. She often participated in musical events in Douglas in the summertime, and was one of the principal performers at an afternoon tea hosted in 1926 by Lenore Spencer and her sister Minnie Belle (Spencer) Gerber. Mrs. Smulski not only sang a vocal solo, but also accompanied some of the other performers on the piano.

In March of 1928 despondent over a severe illness John Smulski shot himself in the head in the family's winter home in Chicago, the Seneca Hotel. He was 61 years old. According to the *Commercial Record*, "John Thomas was called to Chicago Monday on account of the death of J. F. Smulski. Mr. Smulski was a very prominent man in Chicago and has spent his summers on the lake shore for many years. News of his sudden death comes as a severe shock to his many friends here."

Thousands attended his funeral and a long parade of cars followed the casket to the cemetery. According to his biography "He was the only person to whom Chicago paid the supreme honor of dedicating a memorial program in his name. Paderewski himself came to Chicago to pay his respects." The cottage on the Douglas lakeshore was sold shortly afterwards. Mrs. Smulski and her daughter later moved to Arizona, where the mother died in 1947 at the age of 72.

In 1921 Paderewski settled near Paso Robles, California, although he still spent much of his spare time at his villa in Switzerland. When Poland was overrun during World War II, he accepted the presidency of the Polish parliament in exile in 1940. He died June 29, 1941, at the Hotel Buckingham in New York City and his body was placed in a vault in Arlington National Cemetery near Washington D.C. President Franklin D. Roosevelt at that time promised that Paderewski's remains would be returned to Poland "when Poland is free." In 1990 following political changes in the country the people of Poland asked that the American government begin making plans to accomplish this. A committee was appointed by both governments to make arrangements for a 1991 transfer. The hotel room where Paderewski died, including many personal effects, has been recreated at the Polish Museum of America located on Milwaukee Avenue in Chicago, a few blocks from the site of Smulski's bank.

GEORGE COUTOUMANOS
Greek Poet

The beauties of the Saugatuck area have been extolled in poetry for more than 150 years, but George Coutoumanos did it with a difference -- he wrote in Greek.

George Coutoumanos was born on the slopes of Mt. Taygetos in Greece, the son of a shepherd. He came to America at an early age and was employed as a common laborer in Chicago. He and his wife, Jennie, and their five children visited Saugatuck in the summertime for many years and, in 1939, he and Jennie bought a small home and retired to the area.

Although Coutoumanos learned to use the language of his adopted country in ordinary conversation, he continued to write poetry in his native tongue. His poems were first published in the Greek press in the United States, and later three volumes of poetry were brought out in Athens, Greece, to considerable critical acclaim.

In 1961 Warren E. Blake, then head of the Greek department at the University of Michigan called Coutoumanos, "the best Greek poet in America. Athenian publishers give Coutoumanos the same prominence that American editors accord the works of Robert Frost and Carl Sandburg."

There were three volumes of poetry published, *Songs of the Soul*, *The Lullabies* and *Trilogy*. The last of the three was published in 1954 and gives Saugatuck as the place of publication. It is the only English word on an otherwise Greek title page.

Ποίηση
ΓΙΩΡΓΗ ΚΟΥΤΟΥΜΑΝΟΥ

ΤΡΙΛΟΓΙΑ
Ο ΑΓΩΝΑΣ ΤΗΣ ΖΩΗΣ

Ἡ Ἀλήθεια

    Τὸ Ψέμα

        Τὸ Χρῆμα

SAUGATUCK, MICH.
1954

The title page of The Trilogy.

Coutoumanos wrote in classical Greek forms with "rhymed clearly flowing lines" which, Professor Blake told an interviewer, "cannot be easily reproduced in English." In an effort to give some idea of the rhyme and rhythm of the original, John Prevedore translated the first verse of "The White King Cometh, A Saugatuck Landscape":

> Autumn on his arrival brought along
> Mists to the forest, where the trees have shed
> Their many colored leaves, on pathways spread,
> So that the White King may upon them tread.

Coutoumanos used the old forms but with a modern twist. One critic commented that he wrote with "a fresh outlook and a bouncing vigor coupled with Hellenic frankness."

George and Jennie (who died in 1942) lived in a small cottage at 139 Hoffman Street, behind the Log Cabin Tavern (later East of the Sun). The building was later razed to make room for a storage area and delivery dock for Oostings furniture store. Devout Greek Orthodox followers, in Saugatuck they attended the Episcopal church. Jennie is remembered as the kindest of ladies; George, in his twenty-plus years of residence in Saugatuck, is remembered fondly as a philosopher, who helped others see the beauty around them.

Wally Peirce, who as a young man provided the motivating force for the Kalamazoo River chain ferry in the summertime, said that Coutoumanos would sometimes come down to the river on nice days, and, if business was slow, go back and forth on the ferry with him. Wally wrote later, "We would talk about beautiful things that surrounded us that he could see and I was tripping over. It was rather like rowing Plato across the river, and coming back with Bernard Baruch."

His first translated poem of the Saugatuck area was published in the *Commercial Record* in 1930, apparently rendered into English with the help of Saugatuck poet F. W. Greiner.

AUTUMN PICTURES OF SAUGATUCK

Sprits of Indians, idols and gods
Silently hover over beautiful Michigan dunes
While muses begin their autumn dance with music and song
And with gaiety
Greet the charming village of Saugatuck.
Pine trees waft their delicate perfume
Over the historic harbor,
Where shy numphs bathe in summer
And nature lovers bow in prayer.
White-capped waves kiss the coast
Of great Lake Michigan.
Winds blow the shifting sands,
Changing old wonders into new beauties.
Falling leaves decorate the earth
With autumn colors
To welcome the White King --
Beloved son of Nature.
The father of dunes,
Old Baldhead,
Moves slowly.
He sees the last of Indian youths
And of white pioneers that yet remain.
The calmly flowing Kalamazoo
Still keeps the mystery of magic nights
While moon and stars join
To yield true love that never dies.
Saugatuck, dear Saugatuck,
Charming dreamland of artists and lovers.

In the spring of 1944 the *Greek-American Tribune* of New York City published a small prose work written by George Coutoumanos called *Saugatuck Art Colony* in several installments. It was considered a new literary style, prose with a touch of poetry. The following year it was translated into English by Rae Dalvin, formerly of Yale University, and found a ready public in Saugatuck.

The opening paragraph sets the scene:

"On a small triangle in WESTERN MICHIGAN, northeast and southwest of the points where the old road meets and kisses the new U.S. 31, stands SAUGATUCK, joined to the small adjacent farm and tourist village of DOUGLAS and bounded northwest by the slow running Kalamazoo River. In the calm, glistening waters of this river, the large new bridge has thrust its stout cement feet, while over it, proudly passes the long, slow-trailing American road. Just about there, and a few square miles around it, rise the most extraordinary beauties and divine pictures, wonderful to the artistic eye of man for their qualities and association. This amazing natural loveliness exists on no other point in the land, and in all probabilities exists on no other corner of the globe. . . there. . . on this tiny geographic and artistic triangle where nature scatters her priceless artistic treasures, is found the lovely village that today is a great and glorious ART COLONY."

The small book, only 17 pages, goes on to list in some detail the geographical and historical features of the area including the old harbor, "the waters imprisoned for many years, seem like a peplum of sorrow, as if they fell inside and were blurred by the muddy tears of the old piers"; Singapore, "the buried city, the Pompeii of the STATE OF MICHIGAN where the North winds with the foamy waves groan in stormy nights and the hills all around it echo weeping for the complete loss and the unexpected destruction"; and the dunes, "the undulating sand beds sparkle like the canvasses of some great unknown painter."

He closed the small volume, with an almost Chamber of Commerce fervor for his adopted village:

"There. . . inside and around SAUGATUCK in the new harbor, in the river, on the banks of the river and lake, above the sand banks, in the light, in the shade, in the air, in the water, where the sun eulogizes life and nature gives it health, you imagine strength and hopes are struggling and conquering for their ideals. . . Inside the glistening temple of nature, for health, for joy and the happiness of man, virgin nature will one day open her fairest embrace for all mankind. There the poet, the artist, the intellectual, together with the people, will find the mysteries of art, beauty of soul, faith for their work, and his love close to him. He will find society of humanity, where all people live freely and receive the goodness of life, which are the most superior pleasures and ideals of America. . . The playful spring, the dewy summer, the gentle autumn and the winter clad in white scatter with affection and goodness the rich gifts of the Art Colony, in magnificent SAUGATUCK, where art meets together with intellect and scatters its beneficial gifts to the great and glorious America."

He continued to work well into his eighties, giving poetry readings, occasionally, in Chicago and Detroit, and writing. In 1961 a reporter from the *Detroit Free Press* who visited him in his little bungalow off Butler Street wrote, "Still physically and intellectually vigorous at 84, Coutoumanos continues to produce poetry in the ancient style, writing at an old table in his front room. An alabaster bust of Hermes watches over his left shoulder as he writes."

That same year a short poem, translated by Rae Dalven, was published in the *Commercial Record* :

THE RIVER LAKE KALAMAZOO

O cool little river lake
namesake of your river, of spring sublime
gem of the pretty village, mistress of frills,
adorned by the sun cosmetics of time.

You wear your bridal gown of gold
like some Sand-Dune Bride,
The sky's clouds are your mirror,
and you change, change your face with pride.

Since you sleep in nocturnal blackness
the forests in the wind keep a vigil course,
the waves start a dance in secret,
what wave will first embrace your shores?

My little lake of Kalamazoo you resemble

the Indian girl, an unkissed virgin
who sang in full voice, hallooed
like an exotic Michigan siren.

And I reflecting my sorrow for years
in your crystalline waters deep
joyously sing of your beauties
even in the hours when I sleep.

George Coutoumanos died in the Douglas hospital in November of 1962, following a fall at his home at the age of 86. He was buried by his beloved Jennie.

1

"Άκουσεν ἡ 'Αλήθεια
στὸν οὐράνιό της θρόνο,
Σὰν θλιβερὸν ἀντίλαλο
τὸν ἀνθρώπινο πόνο,
Καὶ τὸν χαώδικο γαλάζιο
οὐρανὸ ρωτάει,
Στ' ἀπέραντο βασίλειό του
βοήθεια ποιὸς ζητάει;

THOR HEYERDAHL
Visit to Harbor View

The March 26, 1948, edition of the *Commercial Record* notes modestly:

Notable Visits In Douglas

Douglas has been the host for the past week of an illustrious guest: the noted young Norwegian scientist and explorer, Thor Heyerdahl, of Oslo, Norway. Capt. Heyerdahl has been on a lecture tour in the United States for the last four months, and in looking for a quiet place to rest and write, was pursuaded by Mr. Benjamin Eddy to accompany him to Douglas. While here, he has lived at "Harbor View," the home of Mr. and Mrs. Thomas Gifford. In the fall, Life Magazine and Readers' Digest printed the story of his adventure, "Our Four Months on An Ocean Raft," and the current issue of Readers' Digest carries an item about him. Sunday afternoon, Mr. Eddy took the Captain on a sightseeing drive about the community; he was very much interested in our Lake Shore and dune region. The Eddy's entertained Mr. Harry Plaagemar of Holland and Capt. Heyerdahl at Sunday supper.

And so it came to be that the final proofs of a Norwegian book about a South Pacific adventure were completed in Michigan on the banks of the Kalamazoo.

Benjamin Eddy, who had been born in Ganges, and brought up in Douglas, was working in Ann Arbor and Detroit and was program chairman for an American Roadbuilders Association meeting in Grand Rapids in March of 1948.

Thor Heyerdahl, whose adventure on a balsa raft in the South Pacific had ended in August of 1947, was in the United States on a lecture tour trying to raise enough money to meet outstanding debts connected with the expedition. He had signed a contract with an American agent for a hundred lectures, one per evening, at $200 each. Heyerdahl was to pay his own travel and hotel expenses. The agent had arranged the bookings with little regard to distance and expense and the tour had been very tiring -- and not especially profitable.

He was scheduled to speak to the convention in Grand Rapids on Friday, and, after the talk, he asked Eddy if he knew of a "quiet place to go" where he might read proofs of a book about the expedition, prior to a meeting in Chicago. Eddy called Thomas and Margaret Gifford of Douglas who sometimes took in summer guests and swiftly made the arrangements. Eddy was on his way to Douglas to visit his family and brought Heyerdahl over from Grand Rapids. He settled him in at the Giffords, introduced him to Fred Koning at Tara restaurant in Douglas where Heyerdahl would be taking most of his meals, and invited him to Beech-Hurst, the Eddy home on Ferry Street for Saturday dinner.

Ben's wife, Esther, recalls that she served ham slices with pineapple, sweet potatoes, and apple pie, and her Norwegian guest, tired of hotels and banquet food, was most appreciative. Instead of talking much about the Kon-Tiki adventure, the dinner conversation centered on World War II and his work with a Norwegian army intelligence unit behind German lines. "It was like a movie to hear him tell it," Mrs. Eddy said.

Following a tour of the area the next day, he again was a guest of the Eddys (this time for a roast beef dinner). Then, Ben Eddy left to go back to work, and Heyerdahl set to work on the proofs at the Giffords.

Thor Heyerdahl working on a manuscript

Thomas Gifford was mayor of Douglas from 1948 to 1950. The Gifford home, Harbor View, was located at the corner of Ellis and Center Streets and had only recently been purchased by them. It was one of the older homes in Douglas having been built before 1900 on property given by Michael Spencer to his daughter, Minnie Belle Spencer after her marriage to D. Milton Gerber. Spencer was the very first settler in Douglas, and the original Tara restaurant was his farmhouse. Gerber was a well-known area businessman and had an interest in the Fruit Growers State Bank, the Douglas Basket Factory, and a large farm in the Swan Creek area. (The Gifford home was destroyed by fire, March 22, 1984, and Gifford, died in the fire.)

Heyerdahl stayed in Douglas less than a week, leaving for Chicago before the weekend. He later sent Mrs. Eddy an autographed copy of the English edition of *Kon-Tiki*.

ROBBY BENSON
Debut at the Red Barn

Many dramatic and musical careers have been launched at The Red Barn Theatre, and its predecessor, the Saugatuck Summer Players, but perhaps the biggest success story is that of Robby Benson, who went on from his theatrical debut at the Red Barn in 1967 to make more than 20 motion pictures.

The summer of 1967 Robby's mother, actress Ann G. Benson, was signed by James Dyas, producer/director of the theatre, to sing the part of Nancy in *Oliver*. Ann had made her Red Barn debut the previous year in a season that included *The King and I* and *The Women*, a play that is especially remembered in the Saugatuck area because 40 women, both local residents and summer visitors, joined the Red Barn company in its production.

Although Robby had appeared in commercials since the age of five and had been one of the children in the chorus of *The King and I* at the Red Barn in 1966, he had shown no particular interest in an acting career. Ann later said she was surprised when he came home from a performance of *Oliver* that they had seen in New York City and proclaimed, "I could do that."

Eleven-year old Robby penned his own letter to Dyas asking for an audition for the part of Oliver in the Red Barn production. Dyas, who already had a boy in mind, was not especially enthusiastic but promised him a chance. Ann said later as they were packing to leave for Michigan she had told Robby that Mr. Dyas was being very nice offering him a chance, and that he would be disappointed when he found out that Robby didn't know the part, and wasn't ready for the audition. Robby seemed genuinely surprised to be told that preparation was necessary. That night he took the script and record and went to his room for two hours. When he came out he knew his lines from the scripts and all of the songs.

In Saugatuck he had an audition along with a number of other boys, and got the title role. Because publicity pictures were taken far in advance of the performance, and the Bensons didn't arrive until shortly before rehearsals began, neither Robby nor Ann are pictured in the newspaper advance stories about the show. The publicity shots show Red Barn regular Bruce Hall who played Fagin, and Jim-Billy Dyas, young son of director Dyas, as the Artful Dodger.

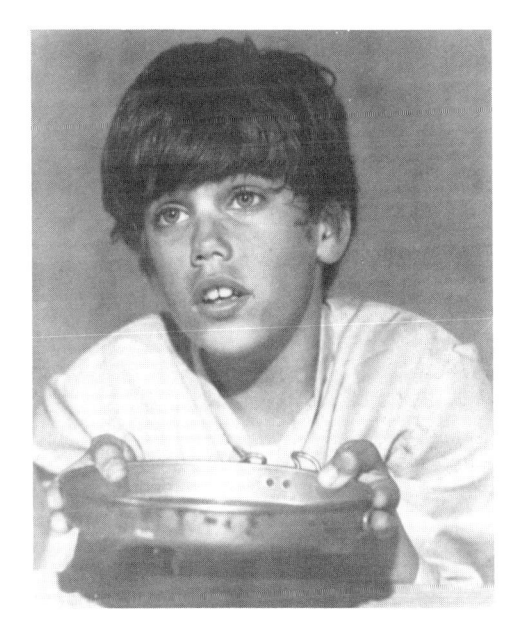

Eleven-year-old Robby as Oliver. This picture was distributed to newspapers the second week of the run.

The advance newspaper stories for the play said that the part of Oliver would be played by "Bobby Segal of New York City." In the program the role of Oliver is played by "Robin Segal", Robby's legal name. Later he would adopt the less formal Robby, and his mother's maiden name, Benson, which she had always used professionally. Ann's husband, and Robby's father, is Jerry Segal, a writer. Daughter Shelli, two years older than Robby, rounds out the family. Shelli is now a fashion designer in California and designs her own line of clothing, J.M. by Shelli Segal, sold at department stores all over the country.

Following the opening performance of *Oliver* on July 18, 1967, the local reviewer wrote:

> Robin Segal as the lonesome and wistful Oliver Twist showed remarkable poise and a nice boy-soprano voice in a professional performance.

The Holland paper lauded him for a "wistful" performance, but noted that Jim-Billy Dyas gave him a "run for the applause" as the Artful Dodger.

His fellow actors helped him with his professional career, Ann recalls. One day Red Barn regular Bruce Hall caught him coming on stage chewing gum. He collared him in the wings, and told him such behavior was not acceptable, "You're working with pros now." Robby especially remembers the summers of 1966 and 1967 because between rehearsals and performances he learned to drive, in a rented Renault in the big Red Barn parking lot off 63rd Street north of Saugatuck.

When they got back to New York after the 1967 Red Barn season Robby was ready to pursue an acting career seriously. His parents sent him to a manager who, after an audition, said he would be interested in handling him.

Shortly afterwards Ann and Robby joined a touring production of *Oliver* that had a four month run in Japan. "We played at the Imperial Theatre in Tokyo," Ann said in a 1971 interview. "The performance was in English but there was an instant translation device at each seat. We lived in a Japanese hotel and would meet all the little Japanese girls outside the stage door and help them with their English homework." The tour went well, except for an earthquake one night in Tokyo.

Robby returned eager to get on with his career. His agent got him some work in commercials, both on camera and as a "voice over", and he became a regular on the daily soap opera, "Search for Tomorrow." By the time he was 15 he was attending school in the morning, filming the soap in the afternoon, and appearing in the Broadway musical *The Rothchilds* in the evening.

While he was still in high school he realized two ambitions: his first feature length film, and at last getting to work with horses for the movie *Jory* in 1972, followed by *Jeremy* in 1973. He attended classes mainly by correspondence.

Since that time he has appeared in a wide variety of movie roles including: the role of a pro skater in *Ice Castles*, as Jack Lemmon's anguished son in *Tribute*, as a gay hillbilly in *Ode to Billy Joe*, as a Chicano gang leader in *Walk Proud*, as a Hasidic Jew in *The Chosen*, as Billy Mills, an American Indian track star, in *Running Brave*, as a retarded lad trying to give his Grandpa the zest for life in *Two of a Kind*, and as Paul Newman's son in *Harry and Son*.

Ann Benson by 1970 had largely given up acting to concentrate on a new career as manager of investment centers for Merrill, Lynch, Pierce, Fenner and Smith. Robby's father, Jerry Segal, accompanied him to movie sets when he was a teenager and during lulls in the filming they would hash over plot possibilities. One of these scripts became the movie *One on One*, about a young high school basketball star's experience when he gets to college. Robby received both star billing and co-writing credit for the film.

In 1982 he took over the lead in the Joseph Papp production of *Pirates of Penzance* on Broadway. Shortly afterwards the female lead was taken over by Karla DeVito. They fell in love and were married in July of 1982 at Karla's home town in Illinois. The couple has one child, Lyric, born in August of 1983.

In 1984 shortly after he finished the movie with Paul Newman, Robby went into the hospital for open heart surgery to repair a defective heart valve. After several months off to recuperate he made a TV movie *California Girls* in 1985.

In 1988 the couple and daughter, Lyric, left California and settled in at the University of South Carolina campus at Columbia, South Carolina, where for two years Robby became artist-in-residence and taught a class in filmmaking. Part of the 1989-90 academic year was devoted to the production of the full length film *Modern Love* which was written, produced and directed by Robby, and which stars Burt Reynolds, Rue McClanahan, Robby, Karla and Lyric, most of the film class, and much of the rest of the population of Columbia. The Bensons returned to California in 1990.

Robby, Karla and Burt Reynolds in a scene from Modern Love.

At 28, after making more than 18 full length movies, Robby mused to a writer: "There are five stages to an actor's career. 'Who's Robby Benson?' 'Get me Robby Benson.' 'Get me a Robby Benson type.' Get me a young Robby Benson.' and 'Who's Robby Benson?'"

He has returned to Saugatuck only once since 1967. In 1971 when his mother was appearing in the title role of *Hello Dolly* at the Red Barn Theatre, both Robby and his father flew in for part of the run.

In interviews Robby freely acknowledges his start at "a summer stock theatre in Michigan" and sometimes even names the town. The details, dates, and ages at which the events occurred often vary from interview to interview. He told one interviewer that his first role was as one of the children in *The King and I* at a "summer stock theatre" when he was five (actually he was 10).

RED BARN THEATRE

The Red Barn logo from a 1967 program.

The Red Barn Theatre had its beginnings in the Saugatuck Summer Players founded in 1948 by Jim Webster. Their plays were presented in the auditorium of the old Saugatuck High School on the hill. In 1951 the troupe moved to their first Red Barn Theatre on Lawn Street in Douglas just down the hill from River Guild (later Gray Gables) on the Blue Star Highway.

In 1953 Webster purchased a large livestock barn on 63rd

Street north of Saugatuck, and converted it into a theatre. The barn had been built in 1921 by John D. Williamson, owner of Belvedere Farms whose elegant house, across 63rd Street was later converted into a retirement home. The animal stalls in the barns became the cast's dressing rooms, the manure pit was scrubbed down and converted into a refreshment stand, and Webster lived in an apartment in the old silo. He sold the enterprise about 1957 to a group of Kalamazoo investors headed by William John Upjohn, and James Dyas was producer-director for 12 years. It also became a teaching theatre with a professional apprenticeship program. During this time the audience area was enlarged to seat 500 patrons, and a new rehearsal stage was added below the new section. Later the Kalamazoo investors hired Ted Kistler, producer-director of the New Vic Theatre in Kalamazoo to conduct a summer season at the Red Barn in Saugatuck. At this time the seats in the house were reduced to 380 with more leg room and a Y-shaped aisle.

The enterprise was sold in 1975 to a group of Illinois and Michigan investors, many active in various community theatre groups. In 1979 and 1980 the Red Barn Theatre was the site of the Gilbert and Sullivan Festival of Western Michigan, a three week program of light operas partially funded by a grant from the Michigan Council for the Arts.

In 1986 the theatre was purchased by Paul Stuart Graham, former producer of Saugatuck's Lakeshore Little Theatre, and renamed the Red Barn Playhouse. The old rehearsal stage on the lower level was improved and enclosed to form the Pavilion Theatre, a small auditorium that could open early, stay open after Labor Day, and be heated if necessary. In 1991 the theatrical tradition of the Red Barn is continuing.

* * * * * * * * * * *

Tom Wopat

Tom Wopat is another western Michigan summer stock actor who made good. He was Luke on the long running television series *The Dukes of Hazzard* and appeared in other movies and plays. For a time he also had his own band. He has returned to the Augusta Barn Theatre near Kalamazoo several times where he was an apprentice in the late 1970's. The story producer-director Jim Ragotzy tells at Augusta is that Tom, as an apprentice, was assigned to build a new outhouse on the hill behind the refreshment stand. Even after modern facilities were installed nearby the old outhouse was retained as a remembrance and conversation piece. When he comes to western Michigan he often visits Saugatuck on his days off. On one visit about 1985 he was traveling on his motorcycle near Wicks Park when a motorist backed out of the angled parking on Water Street striking Wopat's motorcycle. Tom was only slightly injured, but a girlfriend riding behind him on the seat was taken by ambulance to Holland Hospital with more serious injuries including a broken leg.

* * * * * * * * * * *

A TRAVELER'S PREVIEW

A new series of guide books for the traveler who would like to truly see and experience the places he tours. Featuring first-hand practical advice to the tour member or independent visitor.

AUSTRALIA: A TRAVELER'S PREVIEW

The land downunder, where it is warm in the north and cool in the south; the trees keep their leaves but shed their bark; and the animals have big pockets.

GALAPAGOS ISLANDS: A TRAVELER'S PREVIEW

Both natural and historical background on the "enchanted isles," 600 miles off Ecuador in South America.

FIJI: A TRAVELER'S PREVIEW

The south sea island paradise, with miles of beaches, splendid fishing, colorful coral reefs, and a friendly native population that speaks English.

WINTER ON SPAIN'S COSTA DEL SOL: A TRAVELER'S PREVIEW

The southern coast of Spain is gaining popularity as a winter haven from the cold weather of North America. When to go, why, and what to see.

Coming soon: Yugoslavia, Russia

Written from first-hand experience by Art and Kit Lane
Paperback, illustrated.....................$5.95
(Plus 80 cents shipping)

John Allen: Michigan's Pioneer Promoter

John Allen came to Michigan in 1823 and touched many communities. He was co-founder of Ann Arbor, and promoter of Lawrence, Spring Arbor, Lansing, Grand Haven, South Haven, and Richmond in Allegan County. He was an early state senator and was considered for governor.
By Kit Lane   224 pages, illustrated, 5 1/2 x 8 1/2

Hardcover Edition $19.50
Paperback $11.50
        (Shipping $1)

River and Lake
A Sesquicentennial History of Allegan County

By Joe Armstrong and John Pahl
---pages, illustrated, 8 1/2/ x 11 hardcover $26.50
        (Shipping $3)

Western Allegan County History

Kit Lane, editor
537 pages, illustrated, fully indexed, hardbound with full color painting on cover $64.50
        (Shipping $4.50)

Beyond b., m., and d: A Guide to Collecting
and Publishing Family History

Family history should start, not end with the statistics, the b. (born), m. (married), and d. (died). It is important to record the stories that explore the question of who these people were, what they looked like, how they lived. This guidebooks helps the family historian collect the information and prepare it for limited edition printing.
By Kit Lane
52 pages, saddlestitched $4.00
        (Shipping 80 cents)

ALSO AVAILABLE FROM PAVILION PRESS

The Day the Elephant Died and Other Tales of Saugatuck

The first in the Saugatuck "Tales" series. Includes stories of the Singapore bank, murder on main street, battling the Air Force for the radar dome, the day the elephant died and others.
    72 pages, illustrated, 5 1/2 x 8 1/2, paperback $5.50

Singapore: The Buried City $2.00
    24 pages, illustrated, 8 1/2 x 11, indexed, softbound

Saugatuck: A Brief History, Illustrated $2.00
    20 pages, many photos, 8 1/2 x 11, softbound

Shipwrecks of the Saugatuck Area $2.00
    20 pages, illustrated, 8 1/2 x 11, softbound

Douglas: Village of Friendliness $2.00
    28 pages, illustrated, 8 1/2 x 11, softbound

Some Stories of Holland Harbor $2.00
    20 pages, illustrated, 8 1/2 x 11, softbound

Fennville: The Early Years $3.00
    52 pages, illustrated, 8 1/2 x 11, softbound

Fennville: Village to City $3.00
    60 pages, illustrated, 8 1/2 x 11, softbound

Fennville Area $3.00
    64 pages, illustrated, 8 1/2 x 11, softbound
              By Kit Lane

Piers, Pancakes & People $9.00
History of Glenn by Jeanne Hallgren, 63 pp., 8 1/2 x 11, softbound, indexed.

($1 shipping for first book, 50 cents each additional book)